*Happy 12th president to
Charlie from*

TEXAS HISTORY
MOVIES

Published by

The Texas State Historical Association

and

The Texas Educational Association

INTRODUCTION

History takes many shapes. It is stories that we tell about ourselves. It is the record of our past which we reconstruct in ways that will give significance to that past. It forms the webs of meaning that we spin around our lives. History is told at the campfire and dinner table, and is footnoted in scholarly tomes. It flickers like heat lightning across movie and television screens, and then is gone. It is stored—forever, we believe—in computers' memories. But history assumes new shapes and takes on new meanings each time that the stories are retold. And it must be constantly retold to meet the demands of new times, new experiences, new generations.

For several generations of Texans, some of the most vivid and memorable history of the state was found in *Texas History Movies.* This oddly titled work told the stories of Coronado, LaSalle, Austin, Crockett, and Houston in cartoon form. The Alamo, San Jacinto, and the Civil War came to life in a comic book. *Texas History Movies* is history in an unconventional form, but for more than three decades—from the late 1920s to the late 1950s—it was how many Texans learned about their past. By the 1960s, *Texas History Movies* was discontinued, but not forgotten. Its cartoon images lived on in copies in used book stores and in attic trunks. They also lived on in many Texans' minds—indelible images of their ancestors' lives.

In 1974 the Texas State Historical Association thoroughly revamped this well-known cartoon history series and published 100,000 copies under the new title *Texas History Illustrated.* The TSHA, the state's oldest learned society, is a private, non-profit, educational organization which has been involved in the study, research, and publication of Texas history since 1897. So it was appropriate that the Association was responsible for the revision of this off-beat classic that has been read and loved by thousands of Texans.

Texas History Movies is now six decades old, and the Texas State Historical Association has been involved with it for a quarter of a century. In the fall of 1926, the Dallas *News* began running a daily comic strip with the unusual name *Texas History Movies,* which presented the state's history in a humorous cartoon format. The idea for the cartoon series originated with E. B. Doran, director of news and telegraph, and later business manager, of the Dallas *News* and the Dallas *Journal.* Doran carefully supervised and scrutinized the project—the superb cartoon illustrations of Jack Patton, and the text and captions written by John Rosenfield, Jr. J. F. Kimball, former superintendent of schools in Dallas, gave the series its memorable title.

The clever, idiosyncratic cartoons that made up *Texas History Movies* captured the imagination of generations of Texans, but a great deal of the cartoons' charm and humor was found in the frequent use of slang, colloquial expressions, and anachronisms. One series of cartoon panels, for example, shows Stephen F. Austin and friends on their way to Mexico City in 1821 seeking confirmation of a land grant title. They are attacked suddenly by Comanches, and as Austin is pulled from his horse, he cries out, "Hey, what's the big idea?" In the next panel, where we see the travellers tied to a tree by wildly dancing Comanches, Austin's companion comments glumly, "Our goose is cooked." This is not history in the traditional mold. *Texas History Movies* is frequently comic, and even irreverent, but at the same time it joyously celebrates the state's long and dramatic history. It is history with a wink and a nudge—history in a rough, vernacular vein—but history that is appropriate to Texas. And it has had a significant impact on several decades of Texas schoolchildren.

The P. L. Turner Co., Publishers, acquired the copyright to *Texas History Movies* and published the newspaper cartoons in an oversized hardcover book in 1928. At the same time, Magnolia Petroleum Co. arranged with the Turner company to have *Texas History Movies* printed in a paperback booklet to be distributed to schools throughout the state. For three decades this cartoon paperback taught Texas history to thousands of schoolchildren. In 1943 Magnolia acquired the copyright to this extremely popular booklet, although the Turner Company retained the rights to the larger hardback book. By the late 1950s, objections were being raised to some of the drawings and dialogue that stereotyped Indians, Mexicans, and black people. As a result, the Socony-Mobil Oil Co., Inc., successors to Magnolia Petroleum, discontinued *Texas History Movies*. Mobil realized the historical value of the publication, however, and in 1961 assigned the copyright for *Texas History Movies* to the Texas State Historical Association.

The TSHA recognized that *Texas History Movies* contained some good history, that it was of interest to a great many people, and that it had the potential to be a valuable educational tool if revised properly. In 1974 the Houston *Chronicle* approached the TSHA about printing *Texas History Movies* as part of its plan to develop an educational program. The *Chronicle* agreed to print 50,000 copies for the TSHA. Before reprinting the volume, however, the TSHA put together an advisory board with Hispanic and black members. For three months in 1974, this panel carefully examined the work. Anything that was found to be offensive in the drawings or text was deleted or changed. Historical errors in the text were also corrected, and it was published and copyrighted under the title *Texas History Illustrated* to differentiate it from the earlier editions. The finished product was sold to schools at a minimal price to ensure wide distribution. This printing quickly sold out, so the Texas Educational Association, a private foundation, gave the TSHA a grant to print another 50,000 copies. All 100,000 copies of *Texas History Illustrated* have been distributed since 1974, and not one complaint has been received. The Association recently received another grant from the Texas Educational Association to reprint this edition of the book. Although the Association decided to return to the original title, *Texas History Movies*, for this printing, it is the 1974 revised edition.

In the Austin *American Statesman* of April 11, 1985, editor Arnold Rosenfeld wrote a column about *Texas History Movies*, which he had read as a schoolboy. As his column noted, various racial and ethnic groups are caricatured broadly in the original *Texas History Movies*, but this does not make it "a wretched source" of history. Every generation rewrites history according to its own experience, and most history reflects the values of its day. Therefore, *Texas History Movies*, with its biases and caricatures, is a valuable historical artifact that lets us see how we used to understand ourselves and our history. In the 1970s when the TSHA revised *Texas History Movies*, times and values had changed. What was once accepted by many as good humor had become offensive to most people. Appropriate changes were made. This edition of *Texas History Movies* is still Texas history with the bark on. It is still full of loony quips and comic drawings. But with the revisions, it is more appropriate to the times.

As we enter Texas's sesquicentennial era and look back at our experience, we must look back with understanding. For it is by understanding our complex past that we can come to terms with our current flaws and chart our course into the future.

George B. Ward
Texas State Historical Association

IN 1492, CHRISTOPHER COLUMBUS DISCOVERED AMERICA.

IN MARCH, 1493, CHRISTOPHER COLUMBUS PRESENTED INDIANS AND NEW WORLD TREASURES.

IN 1519, CORTEZ CONQUERED MEXICO, DISCOVERING GOLD AMONG THE AZTEC INDIANS.

HOUSES THERE ARE BUILT OF PRECIOUS STONES

BY 1525, ALL EUROPE WAS TALKING ABOUT THE TREASURES OF THE NEW WORLD.

Columbus seeking a new route to India, discovered America in 1492.
Anglo settlement of Western Hemisphere began shortly thereafter.

STORY OF THE LONE STAR STATE

DISCOVERY AND EXPLORATION

Until 1492, America was as remote from Europe and Asia as if it had been on another planet. More than ten thousand years before, the ancestors of the people we call the American Indians crossed over from Asia. Slowly they made their way southward from the Bering Straits, some stopping by the wayside, while others pushed on toward the South. Eventually North, Central, and South America were peopled by their descendants.

Some of these Indians developed remarkable civilizations, especially those who settled in what is today Mexico. The Aztecs, in the region around the City of Mexico, had a well-organized government and were surrounded by ancient Indian buildings when strange white men came to tell them of the wonders of Europe. Further south, in Yucatan, lived the Mayas, a people whose culture was probably finer than that of the Aztec, but who, in 1492, were no longer as important as they had been.

A SPANISH EXPEDITION TO FLORIDA MET HOSTILE INDIANS.

THE SPANIARDS SAILED FROM FLORIDA IN FIVE BARGES.

TWO OF THE BARGES WERE WRECKED ON GALVESTON ISLAND.

YOU HUNGRY— ME HELP.

MOST OF THE SPANIARDS DIED.

In 1528, a Spanish expedition under Narváez reached Florida. The
expedition was marked for disaster.

In the Andes Mountains of South America lived the Incas, whose magnificent stone buildings still amaze the visitor to Peru. In the portions of North America which later became the United States, there were Indians of all sorts and of all degrees of culture; but none of these tribes had advanced as far toward civilization as their kinsmen to the south. In the islands of the Caribbean Sea lived still other Indians, not very powerful in warfare and not very rich in civilization. America was their world. They knew no more of Europe than Europe knew of America, and they were content to let matters remain so. There is no reason to think that the American Indians would have given a penny to learn about the rest of the world. The comforts and advantages of European civilization could have had little meaning for them. They were willing to remain Indians.

But during the centuries that the Indians had lived in America, white men were building up in Europe a civilization. The Christian religion had become their faith. All over

BUT CABEZA DE VACA LIVED AND TRADED WITH INDIANS.

CABEZA DE VACA FOUND THREE OTHER SURVIVORS.

CABEZA DE VACA AND FRIENDS HEALED MANY SICK INDIANS.

IN 1536, CABEZA DE VACA FINALLY REACHED MEXICO CITY.

Cabeza de Vaca escaped and met three of his friends who survived. For two years they walked across Texas and northern Mexico before finding other Spaniards.

Europe, churches and cathedrals and monasteries pointed their spires toward heaven, and devoted men and women worked to educate the people in the ways of the Lord, and to prepare their souls for heaven. Kingdoms had been organized—England, Portugal, Spain—and by 1492 the inhabitants of each kingdom felt themselves superior to the people in the other states. Universities at important towns were training priests and teachers, and advancing the store of human knowledge. People who were living in Europe in 1492 did not realize that one of the most important events in all history was about to take place. Their daily life was about the same, day after day, as it had always been. To them there was no such place as America. They could not have been curious about a place they had never even dreamed of.

So in 1492 America and Europe were still as separate and as unaware of the existence of the other as are Jupiter and Mars. Then came an accident which changed everything.

On a fine day late in that year, the Queen of Castile, one of the kingdoms of Spain, was in a remarkably good humor.

ABOUT 1530
FRANCISCO DE CORONADO HEARD TALES OF WEALTH IN THE NEW WORLD.

CORONADO DECIDED TO SEEK HIS FORTUNE IN AMERICA.

IN 1535 HE SAILED TO MEXICO WITH VICEROY MENDOZA.

THERE CORONADO ENJOYED A HAPPY MARRIAGE AND POLITICAL SUCCESS.

Coronado's voyage to the New World.

She and her husband, who was King of Aragon, had just finished conquering the Moors. These people had overrun the Spanish lands in 711, and for more than seven hundred years the Christian people of Spain had been trying to force the invaders back to Africa. Now they had achieved success. The world looked rosier to Queen Isabella and King Ferdinand than it had ever looked before. They remembered an Italian sailor named Christopher Columbus, who had been appearing at their court at intervals since 1486, trying to interest the monarchs in a scheme for reaching the East by sailing west. Columbus appeared at court in Santa Fe, near where the last battle with the Moors had been fought, once more to explain his project. The matter was soon arranged. The Queen agreed to give Columbus the commission he asked for and invested a small sum in the venture. It was the best investment she, or any other person, ever made.

CORONADO LED AN EXPEDITION TO FIND THE 7 CITIES OF CIBOLA. ONE PARTY SAW THE GRAND CANYON.

THE EXPEDITION WINTERED NEAR THE PRESENT SITE OF ALBUQUERQUE.

WHEN CORONADO REACHED THE RIO GRANDE THE PECOS INDIANS, THROUGH A GUIDE, PLOTTED TO LURE HIM TO THE PLAINS OF TEXAS AND MASSACRE THE OUTFIT.

HE FOUND NO TREASURES BUT ONLY CACTUS AND SAND.

Coronado just evades an Indian plot to kill him.

But what was Columbus' scheme? Was he trying to prove that the earth was round? Did he know that America existed? Did he simply want to explore the Ocean Sea, as he called the Atlantic? Or was he trying to find a new route to the mysterious East, which produced spices, rubies, and all sorts of precious things? We are sure that he, as well as everybody else in Europe who had studied the matter, believed that the earth was round like a ball. More than a thousand years before his time, the geographers had said that one could sail from Europe due west to India, and philosophers had dreamed of the day when a New World would be discovered in the mysterious ocean that lay between the western shores of Europe and the eastern shores of Asia. Columbus may have not known about the story of the New World, but he did know of the writings of the geographers. No one had yet proved that what they had said was true, but all educated people believed it. But these educated people made one great error which was to cause Columbus trouble. They thought that the earth was much smaller than it is. According to their calculations the shores of Asia should have

CORONADO LED HIS MEN NORTH TO THE PRESENT KANSAS-NEBRASKA BOUNDARY.

DISAPPOINTED HE FORCED HIS GUIDE TO CONFESS THE PLOT.

CORONADO EXECUTED THE GUIDE.

I HEREBY CLAIM "QUIVIRA" IN THE NAME OF THE LORD AND HIS MAJESTY THE KING OF SPAIN

("QUIVIRA" - LAND OF TREASURE) IN OCTOBER 1541, CORONADO CLAIMED THE LAND FOR HIS KING.

In 1541, Coronado claimed Texas for the King of Spain.

---

been about where the western shore of Mexico is. He was willing to be the first to demonstrate that one could reach Asia by sailing westward, but his main idea was to find a new route to the rich lands of Asia and, incidentally, to claim for Castile any new lands that he found on the way.

For centuries, ever since the Crusades, Europeans had demanded more and more of the goods of the East. For a long time the cities of Italy had been growing rich from this trade. In recent years, the Portuguese had been trying to find a route around the continent of Africa to these Spice Lands, in order to make their country the market place of Europe. Now, if Columbus could find a route for Spain before Portugal succeeded in establishing her route, this rich trade would make Spain the greatest country in Europe, and Columbus the most important man in the world.

The first voyage of Columbus was full of adventure, and more than once the sailors were ready to turn back before they found land. Columbus himself, in spite of the bold

LA SALLE SAILED MATAGORDA BAY...

EXPLORED WILD AND STRANGE COUNTRY ON FOOT.

LA SALLE'S MEN WERE FASCINATED BY THE BUFFALO.

LA SALLE MADE SEVERAL TRIPS TO EXPLORE THE AREA.

Thinking Matagorda Bay was the mouth of the Mississippi, La Salle searched for a site for his fort.

front which he presented to his men, must have begun to wonder if he had sailed in the right direction when, on October 12, land was sighted. Commanders fell on their knees while the crews chanted *Gloria in Excelsis Deo*. Flags were run up and guns fired. Columbus, who knew how to act a part, dressed himself in armor and threw over his shoulders the crimson mantle of an Admiral of Castile before he stepped ashore. Then, with the royal banner grasped in his left hand, he bent low to salute the earth. When the crew had gathered around him, he drew his sword and, in loud tones, proclaimed the island a possession of the Spanish sovereigns, Ferdinand and Isabella.

On to Cuba and Santo Domingo the explorers went, claiming each of them for Isabella, and giving to each a fine Spanish name. Cuba, he felt sure, must be the mainland, and Cathay and the Great Khan could not be far away. If his guess had been correct, he would have established the direct route to the fabled East for which Portugal was still looking. But, although he sent men inland with a letter of introduction which Isabella had given him, the Great Khan was nowhere to be found. Santo Domingo, he thought, might be

TEXAS ROADS WERE BAD.

WHERE DID THIS RIVER COME FROM? IT IS NOT ON THE MAP

FOUND ANOTHER RIVER. IT WAS THE COLORADO.

LA SALLE STUDIED HIS GEOGRAPHY.

BOYS, I DON'T KNOW WHERE WE ARE. WE'D BETTER RETURN TO THE FORT

EXPLORERS TURNED BACK.

La Salle heads party to explore what he thought was the mouth of the Mississippi.

Cipangu, as Japan was then called by Europeans. We know, of course, that Columbus was mistaken; but he never found it out. When he died in 1506 he was still firm in his belief that he had touched the shores of Asia, although he had made three additional voyages to the Caribbean region.

The discoverer lost little time in getting back to report his find. Pausing only long enough to collect specimens of the products and the people of the region, he set sail for home in the middle of January, 1493. His vessel was blown out of **her** course by hard winds. In March he found himself at a

Portuguese port instead of one of the Spanish harbors. Columbus did not like Portugal. He had tried for years to interest the King of that country in his scheme, but had failed. Now he was invited to visit the King, and after some hesitation, he went. One can imagine the glee with which he told the ruler of the success of his expedition, and we should not blame him if he stretched the truth in the telling. "O man of miserable understanding," the King is reported to have said to himself after he heard the tale, "why didst thou let an undertaking of such great importance go out of thy hands!"

DUHAUT FEARED LA SALLE'S ANGER AND PLANNED TO PROTECT HIMSELF.

DUHAUT FIRED...

AND SO LA SALLE DIED.

LA SALLE WAS BURIED IN TEXAS. NO ONE KNOWS JUST WHERE.

Next morning La Salle came to the spot where his men had fought.

Columbus had already written a report of his expedition and sent it on to Queen Isabella; and as soon as he could he presented himself at the royal court of Castile. He received a royal welcome at the port, and he traveled to court under a splendid guard. A half dozen of his Indians, wearing gold armaments and carrying spears and arrows, and a squad of Spanish sailors, bearing aloft forty gorgeous parrots and all sorts of plants and animals, marched before the Admiral Columbus. Then, sitting at the feet of the monarchs, the dis-

coverer of America told his matchless story. The amazed rulers and the attendants at court then offered up a prayer of thanksgiving and ended the ceremony by marching to the royal chapel for *Te Deum.*

America had been discoverd. Europe soon learned of Columbus' voyage, and the tales that were passed about painted the new lands in such attractive colors that it was impossible to find vessels to carry all of the people who wanted to go out. It was some years before Europe knew *just what it*

TEJAS INDIANS GREETED PRIESTS WITH JOY NEAR PRESENT-DAY CROCKETT.

YOU WANT HOT TAMALE?

THE SPANIARDS DINE ON TEXAS FOOD FOR FIRST TIME.

IT TOOK 3 DAYS TO BUILD THE FIRST CHURCH IN TEXAS, SAN FRANCISCO DE TEJAS.

INDIANS WERE TAUGHT CHRISTIANITY.

As a result of De León's trip to Texas, the Spaniards decided to establish missions and military posts in the country.

was that had been discoverd, but everybody knew that it was a richer land by far than Spain. Columbus, poor man, not only failed to realize the true importance of his discovery, but he died a poor man in spite of the great promises that Isabella had made him.

The islands of the Caribbean were soon filled with Spaniards, eager to find gold or other forms of wealth that could be shipped to Spain. Santo Domingo had seventeen chartered towns by 1513, and there were settlements in Cuba and

Porto Rico also. Still the Spaniards came. Some Spaniards had been shipwrecked on the coast of Mexico and the Governor of Cuba decided to send an expedition to look for them and incidentally to see if there was any rich country in that direction. Hernán Cortés, a young Spaniard who had been in the Indies since 1504, was placed in charge of the expedition. Eleven vessels carried 508 soldiers and 109 sailors toward the mainland early in February, 1519. On the coast of Yucatan they found Aguilar, one of the shipwrecked Span-

After the missions were abandoned in 1693, Spain was contented with
a few presidios or forts near Texas.

iards, who had been there long enough to learn the Mayan language. They took him along as they explored the coast of present day Mexico. At another place, farther north, an Indian chief gave Cortés as a present twenty Indian girls. Among them was one, called Doña Marina, who knew Mayan as well as the language spoken by the Aztec people in the Valley of Mexico. Now Cortés could talk with the Indians. He would speak in Spanish to Aguilar. Aguilar would translate it into Mayan for Doña Marina, and Doña Marina would tell the

Indians, in Aztec, what Cortés wanted. None of the early explorers had such a good system for communicating with the natives.

By the time Cortés and his party had reached the site of modern Vera Cruz, they had learned that Mexico was far richer than any land the Spaniards had yet explored. He had no authority to conquer this country, nor found a settlement; but the Governor of Cuba was no longer Cortés's friend, and before long someone might be sent out to relieve him of

In 1713 the French Governor of Louisiana sent Louis St. Denis to
Texas to establish trade routes.

command. If Cortés wanted to be the conqueror of this rich land, he must act quickly. He did. He scuttled his ships and organized his men into a town government which he called the Rich City of the True Cross (Villa Rica de Vera Cruz). Now the men had to fight under Cortés or be killed by the Indians. Good news reached them. Not only was the Aztec Empire rich beyond description, but there were political troubles in the land. By skillful action, Cortés was able to make alliance with the enemies of the Emperor Montezuma,

and with their aid reached the long bridge which led to Mexico City. There Montezuma met him, placed a gold chain around his neck in token of friendship, and invited him and his warriors into the city. It was a poor day's business for the Aztecs. The Spaniards watched their chance, started a fight, and, although they were at first forced to leave the city, they finally broke the power of the Aztecs. This was in 1521. The Spaniards then took possession of all of the lands Montezuma had ruled over.

*St. Denis' romance complicated international relations. The
government threw St. Denis in jail in Mexico City.*

There are not many passages in all history more marvelous than this capture of a great empire by a mere handful of men. The difficulties which existed in the Empire before the Spaniards came aided, of course, but credit also should be given to the terror caused by Cortés's horses. These Indians had never seen a horse, and the sight of a man in shining armor mounted on such a beast was something they could not understand. They thought the man and horse were one animal--an animal that could shoot with guns. The neck of the horse, they said, was "clothed with thunder"; "the glory of his nostrils was terrible"; and they were sure that "he swallowed the ground with fierceness and rage, and said among the trumpets 'ha ha!' " Without his horses, Cortés, with all his ability, could hardly have succeeded.

Cortés had heard that the Aztec Empire was rich, but he did not dream that it could be as rich as it turned out to be. Gold, precious stones, all sorts of metal, the most magnificent fabrics and intricate designs made of feathers, all sorts of implements, and houses as comfortable and convenient as those of Spain--all of these things, and more, he found when

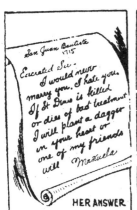

*Monclova, 1715 — My Dear Mañuela: If you will marry me, I will set St. Denis free.
If you don't I will kill him. Yours devotedly, Gaspardo de Anaya.*

he reached the capital city of the Aztecs. Gifts to the King were sent to Spain to insure his favor, and as soon as Cortés had time he wrote long and interesting reports of what he had done. This is important, because no one had authorized him to make this conquest, and if the King should happen to order it, Cortés's head would have been chopped off. The surest way to save his head was for Cortés to convince the King that he was the most valuable subject in the New World, and that the land he had won was the richest in the universe. Fortunately the gifts and the letters arrived in time to convince the King of these things. Cortés was safe, and Mexico belonged now to Spain. But the chief importance to us of the success of Cortés is that his conquest was the first real step toward the discovery and settlement of Texas.

It was to be nearly two hundred years, however, before the King of Spain became interested in Texas sufficiently to take possession of it. It is nearly a thousand miles from Mexico City to the Rio Grande. South of Mexico City lay Central

After his release in Mexico City, St. Denis started back to San Juan.
Bautista to claim Mañuela as his bride.

America and South America. At various places there precious metals were discovered by the Spaniards, and mines were opened. This flow of gold made it possible for Spain to become, for a time, the greatest power in the world. Texas was not only far away, but it had no great mineral deposits. Texas could wait.

But occasionally the Spaniards heard of the Texas country. In 1519, while Cortés was beginning the conquest of Mexico, a Spaniard named Alonso de Piñeda explored the Gulf of Mexico from Florida to Vera Cruz. Piñeda was one of the first white men to see Texas.

ADVENTURES OF CABEZA DE VACA

Again, in 1528, about two hundred Spaniards found themselves shipwrecked on Galveston Island. Some of them got away, but a few of them were held captive by the Texas Indians for six years. The most important man among these Spaniards was one called Alvar Núñez

A Letter to the King, 1727 — If we expect to hold on to Texas we must populate it with civilians and not with priests and soldiers. Please send over four hundred Spaniards.

De Aguayo, Governor of Coahuila.

Cabaza de Vaca, which means literally Alvar Núñez of the Cow's Head. He belonged to an important family in Spain, and had come out to the New World as treasurer of an expedition to Florida. The Florida expedition, which was under the command of Narváez, was a miserable failure. The Indians there were hostile after they found out what the Spaniards wanted, and the great gold deposits the Spaniards had heard of could not be found. The men got separated from their ships, and would have perished in

the wilderness but for the suggestion of one of them that they build boats and try to reach a civilized settlement.

The sea was their only hope. They killed their horses for food, and built a fleet of horsehide boats, in which they hoped to reach Pánuco (modern Tampico), Mexico. They had no way of knowing that Pánuco was more than a thousand miles away, but they probably knew that the Gulf of Mexico is not always smooth sailing.

12

Since 1718, there had been a Mission and Fort on the San Antonio River called San Antonio de Béxar. It was regarded as the center of the new country.

There was one carpenter in the company and, Cabeza de Vaca tells us, there were "no tools, nor iron, nor forge, nor tow, nor resin, nor rigging." Blacksmithing tools were improvised, and stirrups, crossbows, and spurs were melted to make nails and axes. Ropes were made of palmetto fiber and horse hair. The men's shirts were sewed together and used as sails. The skins from the horses's legs were removed, tanned, and used for water bottles. While the work was going on, ten Spaniards were killed by Indians, and forty men died of hunger and disease.

At last five little boats were ready to carry the remaining Spaniards across the treacherous water. Not a man among them knew how to manage a boat, and they, therefore, crept along close to the shore. Some of the men died in the boats as they went along; a few were killed by Indians when they went ashore to get food; and when they came to the mouth of the Mississippi, the boats became separated. Cabeza de Vaca had advised Narváez, who was commander,

1801 — Nolan reached the Brazos River near the present site of Waco, where buffalo, elk, deer, and horses were plentiful.

---

how to avoid some of the misfortunes, but Narváez would not heed the warning.

Two of the boats were wrecked on Galveston Island on November 6, 1528, and a third and fourth vessel were wrecked on the Texas coast to the west. Narváez, in the fifth boat, continued westward, but after he had landed his men ashore, and was preparing to spend the night in his boat with his page, who was ill, a sudden wind swept the frail craft into the sea. He was never heard of again.

Cabeza de Vaca's name has become a household word in Texas, because he was the first European to explore the country. But it should be understood that he had not intended to visit Texas, much less explore it. His first thought was to get away. The Indians among whom he and his companions found themselves, however, had other plans for the strange white men that the sea had brought them.

When they reached Galveston Island, the Spaniards were near to starvation and many of them were ill, so

13

March, 1801— The party en route to Nacogdoches had to cross the Trinity River.

---

that their bodies looked like "the perfect figures of death," Cabeza de Vaca wrote. The Indians "at sight of what had befallen us, and our state of suffering and melancholy destitution . . . began to lament so earnestly that they might have been heard at a distance and continued doing so more than half an hour." Ill as they were, the Spaniards were impressed by the generous sympathy of these Texas Indians who, though wild and untaught, grieved over a fellow-creature's misfortunes. They carried the Spaniards to their village, lodged them in huts, built fires, and fed them on roasted fish and roots. Until far into the night, Cabeza de Vaca remembered years later, the Indians looked after their comfort, sang and danced and wept about them.

During the winter many of the Spaniards died, for the storms stopped the fish supply and it was too cold to dig for roots. Then, when spring came, an epidemic broke out among the Indians and about half of them died. The Indians were about to kill the Spaniards, thinking that they had brought the plague upon them. One of the chiefs pointed out that the white men died of the disease. If the white men could bring the plague

During the early nineteenth century attempts were made to take Texas from Spain.

---

upon the Indians, they could surely have prevented their own people from dying of it. So, the Indians allowed the Spaniards to live, but they were still inclined to think that they had some divine powers. The Indians, wrote Cabeza, "wished to make us physicians, without examinations or inquiring for diplomas." In vain they protested that they knew nothing of medicine. The Indians said if they would not heal the sick, neither should they eat food.

A few days of hunger convinced Cabeza de Vaca that he might as well do as the Indians wished. He had carefully watched the Indian medicine men, and when he began his work of curing. he followed their plans, with an important addition. "Our method," he wrote, "was to bless the sick, breathing upon them, and recite a *Paternoster* and an *Ave Maria*, praying with all earnestness to God our Lord that He would give health and influence them to make us some good return. In His clemency He willed that all those for whom we supplicated should tell others that they were sound and in health, directly after we made the sign of the blessed cross over them. For this the Indians treated us kindly;

14

October, 1812 — The Gutiérrez-Magee expedition crossed the Colorado at what is now Columbus.

they deprived themselves of food that they might give to us, and presented us with skins and some trifles."

Several times, Cabeza de Vaca was about to leave these hospitable Indians and set out in search for the nearest Spanish settlement; but for nearly six years the Indians would not let him go.

He was occasionally allowed to go over to the mainland to trade with other Indians. His fame as a medical man went before him, and everywhere the Indians received him with honor. But after each expedition to the mainland he returned to the Island, for his companion, named Oviedo,

could not swim; and Cabeza would not leave him. Finally Cabeza de Vaca persuaded his friend to make an attempt to get away. Probably he swam to the mainland with Oviedo on his back, or towed him across on a piece of driftwood. At any rate, the two Spaniards, naked and armed only with bows and arrows, set out from the coast near Galveston. Oviedo, however, fearing the mainland Indians, soon deserted his companion and returned to the island. Cabeza de Vaca continued alone until he made contact with three of his fellow countrymen who had escaped from the island six years before. One of these,

During the Siege of Goliad the shooting ceased.

Estevanico, a Moorish slave, was probably the first Negro to visit this region. The four wandered across a good part of Texas, frequently lost their way, and were in constant danger of capture by Indians. But at length, they were able to reach Culiacán, the northern outpost of Spanish power, on the Gulf of California. Cabeza had been so long without clothing that he found it difficult to dress like a civilized person; and for a long time he could not get used to sleeping in a house.

He eventually reached Mexico City, where he told the story of his wanderings to the Viceroy. The Viceroy wanted Cabeza de Vaca to lead an expedition for him into

this Texas country, but Cabeza preferred to have a commission directly from the King. He, therefore, hurried away to Spain, leaving behind Estevanico, who had made a good part of the trip with him. This black man later told many stories of his adventures, and was sent to show a priest, Friar Marcos, the way to the lands of the North. Estevanico was killed by Indians, but the report of Friar Marcos of the wonders of the Northern country led to the sending out of the first great expedition that touched the soil of Texas. Cabeza de Vaca wrote and had published in Spain an account of his adventures **in Texas.**

GUTIÉRREZ VOTED TO FIGHT. XX

AMERICANS SOUGHT MAGEE.

KEMPER BECOMES COMMANDER.

AMERICANS UNDER KEMPER ATTACK FIRST.

Following Magee's death, Major Kemper took command.

It is the first book about the region, and one of the most interesting volumes ever written.

Friar Marcos, after the death of Estevanico, went as far northward as he dared, hoping to reach the turquoise doors of the Seven Cities of Cíbola. The Indians had told Estevanico of these amazingly rich cities. They said that beyond Cíbola were other provinces, each of which was "a much greater matter than those seven cities." From a plateau, the friar was at last able to see the Indian village of Hawikuh outlined against the Zuni mountains. It must, he thought, be one of the Seven Cities. Before he hurried back to Mexico City to report to the Viceroy, he planted a cross and took possession of the city and all of the cities beyond it in the name of the King of Spain. "I returned with more fear than victuals," he wrote.

CORONADO'S QUEST FOR GOLD

The friar's report of the great riches to the north fitted in with tales the Spaniards had heard from the Indians. The people of Mexico were ready to believe that another land as rich as Mexico had been found. Priests referred to the discovery in their sermons, and the gossip of the barber shops was of little else. Everybody seemed to want to go to Cíbola and grab his share of fabulous wealth.

AT 10 P.M. THE SOLDIERS MARCHED SINGLE FILE.

REPUBLICANS SILENTLY MARCHED WITHIN A FEW FEET OF SPANISH OUTPOSTS.

GUARDS WERE UNAWARE OF THE APPROACHING ARMY.

THE SPANISH ARMY SLEPT SOUNDLY.

June 17, 1813 — Now Colonel Perry led the Republicans toward the Spanish camp on Alazán Creek, near San Antonio.

The problem of the Viceroy was not to get men to go on this expedition, but to select a force of 300 men from the many who begged to go. Francisco Vásquez de Coronado was made commander, and in February, 1540, the Viceroy made the long journey from Mexico City to Compostela, near the Pacific coast, to start the expedition off. No expedition so magnificent had been organized in Mexico, and none had set out with such high hopes. The gentlemen were dressed in shining armor and rode the finest horses the country produced. Behind them marched foot-soldiers, and they were followed by several hundred Indians, in their war-paint. Pack-mules, cannon, and a thousand extra horses were supplied at the royal expense; and droves of cattle, sheep, goats, and hogs were driven along to supply food. Coronado wore an armor made of gold, and at his side rode Friar Marcos in his gray robe of the order of Saint Francis. Ships were sent up the coast of the Gulf of California, carrying supplies for the army.

Through the northern part of present-day Mexico

June 18, 1813 — At daybreak an American lookout saw the Spaniards stirring.

and into Arizona and New Mexico the expedition marched, learning a great deal about this unexplored country, but the Seven Cities of Cibola were not to be found. Disappointed, and determined to find something of importance, the Spaniards were willing to believe the tales of an Indian they called The Turk. This Indian told of a land called Quivira, from which he said he came. This country was rich beyond description. Its ruler was lulled to sleep each day by the music of golden bells hung in a great apple tree. In the rivers swam fish as large as horses. The commonest utensils were made of

pure gold. The Turk was willing to show the Spaniards the way, and the Spaniards were willing to go.

In April, 1541, Coronado started eastward from a place near Albuquerque to find and conquer Quivira. Soon they entered the plains of Texas, where they found huge herds of buffalo, or as the Spaniards called them, "hump-backed cattle." One of the Spaniards was impressed by the fact that the Spanish soldiers, with all their cattle and baggage trains, "in travelling over these plains, would leave no more trace where they had passed than if nothing had been there—nothing—so that it

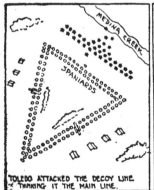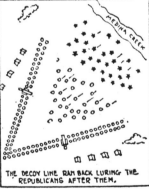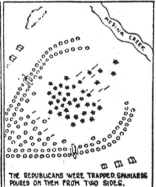

August 18, 1813 — Toledo moved against the Spaniards.

was necessary to make piles of bones . . . so that the rear-guard could follow the army."

Food and water became scarce. Some began to suspect that The Turk had deceived them. Most of the army was sent back to New Mexico, while Coronado and thirty-six men pushed on into the present state of Kansas. When they reached a place near Great Bend, Kansas, The Turk confessed that he had been engaged by the New Mexico Indians to lead the Spaniards out into the plains and lose them. The Wichita Indian towns in Kansas certainly did not correspond with the descrip-

tion of Quivira. "Neither gold nor silver, nor any trace of either, was found among these people," a Spaniard recorded. Coronado had The Turk killed, set up a cross on which he wrote: "Francisco Vásquez de Coronado, general of an expedition, reached this place," and turned back, empty-handed, toward New Mexico.

The expedition which had set out with such high hopes, returned to report that there were no great riches in the region they had explored. For a long time after this failure, no one was anxious to explore the region north of the settled limits of Mexico. Coronado's army

17

The Spaniards executed the captives.

---

had crossed western Texas, but had found there only the sands and scant grass of the plains. At the same time that this expedition was in western Texas, another group of Spaniards came into eastern Texas. These were the remnants of the De Soto expedition which had landed in Florida. After De Soto had discovered the Mississippi River, he died; and the men who were with him tried to find a route through Texas to Mexico. They crossed the Red River near Texarkana and may have gone as far as the Brazos before they turned back. They returned to Mexico by water.

The Spaniards, after 1540, knew of Texas, but had found nothing there which made them believe that the country was very valuable. Texas would have to wait more than a hundred years before Spain undertook to establish settlements there; however, explorations continued.

ESTABLISHMENT OF MISSIONS

After Coronado and his men returned from their long trip to the north country with tales of hardships, everybody in Mexico knew, or thought he knew, that there was nothing of value in the region of Texas.

1790 — The family of Lafitte in Bordeau, France.

But there were missionaries in Mexico who believed that the souls of red men were worth saving, even if those red men had little wealth. The Franciscans were among the most earnest of the missionaries, and while other Spaniards were looking for gold, they were converting Indians at many places north of Mexico City. At San Juan Bautista, on the Rio Grande, they had a very important mission, and at the College of the Holy Cross, farther south, they were training men to work among the Texas Indians. The money for missionary work was supplied by the royal treasury, and it is not

to be wondered at that the government placed the missions "where they would do the most good." That meant, of course, that the government was more anxious to Christianize and civilize rich Indians than those who lived in a poor land, such as the Spaniards thought Texas was. It was partly for this reason that New Mexico was more attractive than Texas.

The Indians of New Mexico were *pueblo* Indians, that is, Indians who lived in villages. Such Indians were more likely to have wealth than the roving Indians of the Texas country. In 1598 a great Spanish expedition,

*Lafitte was commissioned by the Mexican Government to prey upon
Spanish commerce in the Gulf of Mexico and the Atlantic Ocean.*

---

under Oñate, brought New Mexico under Spanish control and established a band of Franciscan missionaries there. In 1609 the town of Santa Fe was founded as the capital of New Mexico. In 1680 the Indians drove the Spaniards out. Many of them, and some of the Christianized Indians, fled to the El Paso region. For the next eighteen years, the Indians held New Mexico. Then Governor Vargas crushed the Indian resistance and made New Mexico once more a Spanish province.

From New Mexico bands of hunters, traders, and missionaries sometimes wandered over into western, and even central, Texas. More than once petitions were sent to the government asking that settlements be made in Texas. But the time had not come for that. The Spaniards had gained control of New Mexico, to the west; and they were doing their best to keep control of Florida, to the east. Texas, a land-in-between, had not appeared to them to be important enough to worry about.

One fine day Jean Lafitte arrived at Barataria.

FRANCE STIRS SPAIN TO SETTLEMENT

Between Florida and New Mexico lay the Mississippi River, which had been discovered by De Soto and his Spanish followers. All of the North American continent was claimed by Spain. But France was anxious to get wealth from the New World, and even though she may have had no legal right to do so, she had explored and made settlements in Canada. In 1673, some of these Frenchmen from Canada found the Mississippi River. A few years later Robert Cavalier de la Salle explored

the river to the Gulf of Mexico. Near the mouth of the great river he erected a post on which he had written: "Louis the Great, King of France and of Navarre, reigns. April 9, 1682." And after the priests had read their prayers, and the soldiers had fired their muskets, and everybody had shouted: "Long Live the King!" La Salle proclaimed that the river and all of the lands drained by it belonged to King Louis XIV of France. If France should actually take possession of this land which La Salle claimed, a wedge would be driven between Spanish Florida and Spanish New Mexico. The

Lafitte considered the British offer of £30,000 and a boat to join His Majesty's Navy.

French might even conquer one or both of these territories from the Spanish.

This threat, as thoughtful Spaniards feared, soon became a reality. After his exploration of the river, La Salle hurried to France and got permission to found a French colony at the mouth of the Mississippi. With priests, soldiers, women, and mechanics, to the number of about three hundred, he sailed from France in the summer of 1684. For some reason, these Frenchmen missed the mouth of the Mississippi and found instead the entrance to Matagorda Bay, on the coast of Texas. This was in

November, 1685. There had been troubles among the Frenchmen on the voyage, and more troubles awaited them. A vessel was wrecked. A ship-load of the colonists returned immediately to France. Too late, it was discovered that the Mississippi River was far away. La Salle made the best of a bad situation.

Timber from the wrecked ship furnished materials for a sort of fort and some huts. The place was called Fort Saint Louis, in honor of an ancestor of King Louis XIV. As time passed and the colonists failed to find a route to French settlements on the Mississippi, or even to Spanish

On April 15, 1817, Lafitte called his aides together on board the schooner Carmelita.

---

settlements below the Rio Grande, the men began to desert their leader and wander away. Smallpox and other diseases took the lives of some of those that remained, and hostile Indians were all about them. All sorts of plots were concocted by these desperate Frenchmen. Finally, as a last resort, La Salle determined to make one more effort to find the Mississippi. He hoped to reach the French settlements far to the north, and secure assistance for his little band. With sixteen companions, the leader set out.

After they had crossed the Brazos River and reached the neighborhood of the present town of Navasota, bitter

quarrels began. Three of the men were murdered by others as they slept, after a dispute over the division of meat. The next day the murderers hid in the tall grass and killed La Salle as he searched for his murdered nephew. The great Frenchman died without a word, while his murderers stood over his body shouting: "There thou liest, great Bashaw! There thou liest!" It was not long before the murderers quarrelled and both were killed. A few others of La Salle's party eventually reached the French settlements.

INDIANS BATHED AT WEST END OF ISLAND.

THE PIRATES TEASED THEM BY STEALING THEIR CLOTHES.

ONE DAY THE PIRATES STOLE THE BEST LOOKING SQUAWS FROM THE INDIANS.

AS REVENGE A BAND OF INDIANS KILLED FOUR PIRATES WHILE THEY WERE ON A HUNTING EXPEDITION.

Tribes of Indians were constant visitors at Galveston, which was renamed Campeachy by Lafitte.

At Fort St. Louis things went from bad to worse. Disease, starvation, and Indian raids combined to wipe out the survivors that La Salle had left on Lavaca Bay.

In Rouen, France, where La Salle was born, a handsome monument has been erected to his memory. He was one of the great men who gave their lives in an effort to create a French empire in the New World. Historic markers that cite the route of his expedition have been erected by Texans who admire his personal qualities and recognize his importance in making the history of Texas.

La Salle planted the first colony of Europeans on the soil of Texas, and this led ultimately to the colonization of Texas by Spain.

It was a long time before news of La Salle's colony reached Spanish officials in Mexico. When they learned that another nation was interested in Texas, that long-neglected region suddenly became very important. They resolved, first, to drive the Frenchmen out, and then to establish missions in Texas to hold the land for Spain. Expeditions were sent by land and sea to search for the

AFTER ITURBIDE TOOK HIS SELF-MADE THRONE, MANY OF THE REVOLUTIONISTS DESERTED HIM.

THE EMPEROR LIVED HIGH.

MEET GENERAL SANTA ANNA. HE TURNED UP AS ONE OF ITURBIDE'S CHIEF SOLDIERS.

THE MEXICAN CONGRESS PROTESTED.

We have shown conditions in Texas. Now we will take up the rule of Iturbide, proclaimed Emperor of Mexico and Texas, with the name Agustín I.

French settlement. One of the sea expeditions found the hulk of a French vessel in Matagorda Bay, but found no Frenchmen on the seas. Three expeditions were sent by land from northern Mexico under Captain Alonso de León, governor of Coahuila. Twice De León returned without having found a trace of the French. On his last exploration, however, in 1689, he carried with him Father Massanet, a Franciscan who had long urged that missions be established north of the Rio Grande. A great many other people went along, too; and an old Spanish soldier

wrote to De León asking that his young son Antonio be allowed to go with the expedition "so that when he is old he will have a tale to tell." This expedition found Indians in Texas who had articles from La Salle's colony — a Bible, and other books, as well as European clothing. Guided by the Indians, the Spaniards found the site of Fort St. Louis. The houses were deserted, and the bodies of Frenchmen were scattered about the prairie.

One of the Indian chiefs invited Father Massanet to bring other priests with him and work among his people.

Iturbide, suspecting the loyalty of Santa Anna, sent a message recalling him from Vera Cruz.

This was exactly what the good father wanted to do, and as soon as he returned to Mexico, he secured permission to undertake the work. Again with Captain De León in command, Father Massanet and a company of soldiers, artisans, and adventurers started northward from Coahuila in March, 1690. Twenty mules carried wine, wax, and other goods needed for the mission chapels, as well as clothing and presents for the Indians. Their route led them by the site of Fort St. Louis. Here the expedition halted while Father Massanet set fire to the ruined houses. On eastward the Spaniards went, to the land of the Téjas. These Indians were not a tribe, but a confederation of several tribes that lived in East Texas. Their word for friend, or ally, was *Téja*; hence, the Spaniards called them the Téjas Indians.

The Indians were friendly, and soon the Spaniards were at work building their first mission in the Texas region. They named it the mission San Francisco de los Téjas, in honor of the founder of the Franciscan order and of the Indians it was to serve. The site selected was about twenty-five miles from the present town of Crockett, not far from the river. When the Spaniards

In July, 1824, Iturbide landed at the Port of Soto la Marina, Mexico.

began cutting down trees for the log building, the Indians gathered around at first to watch, and then to help with the work. In three days, the crude building was finished, and on June 1, 1690, it was consecrated with great ceremony.

A large group of Indians had gathered for the occasion, Father Massanet reported, and they looked on with wonder as the priests in their splendid vestments, soldiers in their uniforms, and other Spaniards in their best suits, marched in the solemn procession carrying symbols of their faith. The Spanish guns roared salutes at intervals, and at the end of the service, Father Massanet hoisted the royal flag of Spain, a banner bearing on one side the picture of Christ and on the other a picture of the Virgin of Guadalupe, patron saint of the Indians of Mexico.

Another mission was established near by, on the Neches River, and when the expedition turned back to Coahuila, three friars and three soldiers were left to hold Texas for Spain. Twenty-six loads of flour, twenty cows, two yoke of oxen, several plows and other implements, as well as nine horses and a supply of ammunition

The Republican Army entered Mexico City and the Generals set out to establish a new government.

---

were left at the missions. Six Spaniards were expected to hold Texas for Spain! The mission on the Neches was soon destroyed by flood, and at San Francisco de los Téjas serious troubles soon developed. Many Indians died of disease, for which they held the priests responsible. Droughts and floods came, and the early friendship of the Indians changed to hostility. One of the priests discovered that the Indians were planning to massacre the Spaniards; and on the night of October 25, 1693, the priests and soldiers buried the mission bells and slipped away toward Mexico.

At the close of the year 1693, Texas belonged again to the Indians. French and Spanish settlements had been founded, but both had failed. The Spanish government was willing to forget about Texas again, if France would only leave the country alone.

That was not to be. France was seriously undertaking to hold the territory of the Mississippi River, which La Salle had claimed for her. In rapid succession she established settlements at Biloxi (Mississippi), Mobile (Alabama), Natchitoches, and New Orleans (Louisiana). She planned to control the Gulf coast and to establish

In 1782 we find Moses Austin, a native of Durham, Connecticut,
engaged in business in Middletown of that state.

---

trade with the Spanish settlements in northern Mexico, as well as to trade with the Indians west of the Mississippi River. If the French plans had worked out, Texas might have become a province of the French king.

There were three Franciscan missions on the Rio Grande, and the missionaries there were as eager to convert the Texas Indians as Father Massanet had been in 1690. One of these friars, whose name was Father Hidalgo, hit upon a scheme which would insure the reoccupation of Texas. He wrote a letter, which eventu-

ally reached the French governor of Louisiana, in which he pointed out the importance of Christianizing the Texas Indians and incidentally mentioned the profit that could be gained from trading with those Indians.

The French governor sent Louis Juchereau de Saint Denis, a dashing young Indian trader, into Texas. He carried with him a stock of goods, and he was instructed to buy cattle and horses, as well as to search for Father Hidalgo. In 1714 he was at Natchitoches, the new trading post the French had established near the Red River.

In 1814, Stephen F. Austin was elected to the House of Representatives in the Missouri State Legislature.

He came on westward, and soon he was among the Indians who remembered the kindly Spanish priests who had lived among them twenty years before. The Indians said that they wanted the missionaries to return, and Saint Denis was delighted to carry their message to the missionaries on the Rio Grande.

When he reached the Rio Grande settlements, Saint Denis was arrested and spent a portion of his time while under arrest courting a relative of the officer who had made him prisoner. At last orders came to send the Frenchman to Mexico City. There he conferred with the Spanish officials, and secured for himself the job of guide and commissary for an expedition. Spain had determined once again to occupy Texas. Again it was the danger of French intrusion that had made Texas seem important. It seems strange that the Spanish should have chosen a Frenchman to guide such an enterprise!

ESTABLISHMENT OF EAST TEXAS MISSIONS

Sixty-five people, including twelve missionaries and

Walking to his lodgings to collect his baggage for a speedy trip out of Texas, according to the Governor's orders, Moses Austin met in the Plaza Baron de Bastrop, a land speculator whom he had met in Missouri.

six families, started out with supplies for farms, missions, and a fort, as well as about a thousand head of cattle. They paused at the site of modern San Antonio to refresh themselves at San Pedro Springs. The missionaries thought that would be an excellent site for missions, and the commander thought it might serve also as the location of a town. But they had not reached the Téjas country, where they were authorized to do their work. On they went, across the Brazos River, into the land of the Téjas. The Indians were delighted to see the Spanish priests among them again. They selected a site for the first mission, and assisted in building it. It was called San Francisco de los Neches, and on July 3, 1716, Father Hidalgo was placed in charge of it. Five other missions were established by this expedition.

At each place, the military commander distributed tobacco, trinkets, and clothing to the Indians, and explained to them that both God and the King of Spain

Just before he planned his departure, Moses Austin paid one last visit to his daughter,
Mrs. J. M. Bryan, who lived at Hazel Run, Missouri.

loved them. In fact, he said, that was the reason that the good friars had come to live among them: to teach them the ways of God and the wishes of the Spanish King.

There were many Indians in the region of these missions, and they were friendly toward the priests; but the work of the missions never prospered. The French were near by, keeping the Indians well supplied with food, and trading with them. Furthermore, the Indians prized their independence. They visited the priests, but most of them refused to live in the mission establishments. Of course, under the circumstances, it was impossible to teach these red men the mysteries of the Christian religion and of European civilization. Until 1730 the five East Texas missions continued their feeble existence. Then three of them were moved to the San Antonio River. The friars at the other two missions continued their work for nearly forty years more, but without success. "The gospel," one of the missionaries consoled himself, "does not command us to convert, but only to preach."

Stephen received a letter from his father informing him that the
Mexican Government had granted permission for the colony.

These East Texas missions are important, not because they were great establishments, but because they demonstrated that Spain had made up her mind to maintain a foothold in Texas.

The mission buildings in East Texas were made of logs, and nothing remains of them today. We are not even sure of the exact site of some of them, but for half a century they stood as a symbol of the determination of Spain to hold Texas, and as a monument to the zeal of the Franciscan friars, who were willing to risk death in order to convert the Indians to the Christian religion.

THE SAN ANTONIO SETTLEMENTS

Another group of Texas missions had slightly better success. Beginning in 1718 the San Antonio River valley became the scene of Spanish activity. One of the missions on the Rio Grande was moved to the San Antonio River that year and renamed San Antonio de Valero. Nearby was established the *presidio* (fort) San Antonio de Béxar to protect the missionaries. Along a twelve

Stephen F. Austin and his party reached San Antonio in August, 1821.

---

mile stretch along the San Antonio River may still be seen the ruins of five missions. San Antonio de Valero, commonly called the Alamo because of the *alamo*, or cottonwood trees that grew there, is now in the heart of the city of San Antonio. The Mission San José de Aguayo, founded in 1720, is four miles away, on the right bank of the river. The carvings and statuary that ornamented its front, and the "rose window" of the baptistry, made its chapel the most impressive of the Spanish buildings erected in Texas. Mission San José has been restored and is maintained as a historic site by the State of Texas.

In 1731 the Concepción Mission, which has stood the ravages of time better than any of the others, was established. Its outside walls were plastered and on the front were painted curious designs in brilliant colors. The San Francisco de Espada Mission, nearby, is sometimes called the oldest mission in Texas, although it was not established at its present site until 1731. But the friars who established it near San Antonio considered it an old mission even then. They were the successors of the missionaries who founded the mission San Francisco de los Téjas in 1690, and those who established San Francisco de los

On March 20, Austin set out for Mexico City with two companions' bound in that direction.
Austin was seeking confirmation of his land grant from the new Mexican Government.

Neches in 1716. So they might claim that their establishment, although new at San Antonio, was the first to be founded in Texas. San Juan de Capistrano, not far away, is another of these east Texas missions which was moved to San Antonio in 1731.

Thus Texas became a Spanish missionary territory. It was less expensive for the King to support missionaries than to garrison Texas with soldiers, and it was also more effective. The Spanish soldiers did not get along well with the Texas Indians, but the friars gained the affection of the red men by gentleness and kindliness. In general, Spain kept only enough soldiers in Texas to protect the mission establishments from attack by hostile Indians. If we may believe what the missionaries wrote about these soldiers, the troops Spain sent to Texas were a sorry lot.

When we look at the impressive ruins of these missions around San Antonio, we are apt to get a wrong impression of what a mission was. In most cases, all that remains of the establishment is the chapel. When

On May 13 Austin succeeded in getting a petition before the Mexican Congress.

the missions were in actual operation, however, the chapel was only one of a great many buildings. The mission was in effect a village in which the Indians lived while the friars taught them "Catholic faith and good manners." The houses in. which the Indians lived and worked, the buildings in which clothing, food, and supplies of all kinds were stored, the chapel, the living quarters of the missionaries, and a good many other buildings were ordinarily enclosed by a high wall. This was not only for protection against attack, but to keep the mission Indians from running away. Every night the Indians were carefully locked in their houses and a guard posted on the wall which enclosed the settlement.

Never—except when they escaped into the woods, as many of them succeeded in doing—were the mission Indians out of the sight of the watchful missionaries. One of these Texas Franciscans wrote in 1729:

"It is necessary that the missionary take them out to the fields to the work of planting, that he go about with them in planting and harvesting, and that he take care that they guard the stock. He must count them, go with them to work on the buildings, and, in short, he must

Austin's colony gave Texas a new lease on life.

accompany them in all their occupations. For experience shows that if the priest leaves the Indians alone, the work is not done, and the Indians themselves flee to the forest. Every day it is necessary to give rations to each Indian, for if the food is left where they can get it, in two days the whole supply is consumed."

Early in the morning, and again at night, they recite the Catechism, and several times a week they were instructed in the mysteries of religion "with similies and arguments adapted to their inexpressible stupidity." When the missionaries felt that an Indian knew the ele-

mentary principles of Christianity, he was baptized, provided he had shown "some disposition to remain at the mission (which not even the oldest Christians have in full measure)." The missionaries gave a great deal of care to the handicrafts of their Indians, and the huge farms which the Indians cultivated under supervision. "They do this," one of the missionaries wrote, "both because it is their duty and because it is the most important means of subsistence for those who live at the mission. The good treatment of the mission Indians," he continued, "attracts those who inhabit the woods.

Food was scarce at first and Austin's colonists had to rustle fodder.

They observe and consider the advantages the others enjoy." The sick Indians were cared for with great care by the priests. Those who were seriously ill were given special food, and all sick Indians were excused from work. "For this reason," one missionary reported, "not a few feign illness and the missionaries, in order to keep them from running away, pretend to be deceived."

Life in the mission was not easy, either for the missionaries or for the Indians. The permanent effect of the devoted work of the missionaries was almost nothing. In 1740 there were 1,700 Indians living in the Texas mis-

sions. In 1785 there were only about 500; and at the end of the Spanish period, in 1821, none of the Indians remained in the missions and the buildings themselves were falling into ruin. The missions failed, then, to accomplish what the Franciscans hoped they would accomplish —convert and civilize the Texas Indians; but they succeeded in making good Spain's claim to the province. Whatever the cost to the King, it was a good investment.

There were other Spaniards in Texas, who were neither missionaries nor soldiers. Most of them lived in San Antonio, Nacogdoches, or La Bahía, cultivating farms

Some of the other colonies prospered and some failed. The most interesting was Edwards' Grant around Nacogdoches, where the new American-Texans first rose in rebellion.

or raising cattle in the neighborhood of the town.

In 1722, after the Marqués of Aguayo had travelled across Texas with five hundred soldiers and 5,000 horses, he recommended that a town be established in the province and that colonists be sent to live in it. A royal order was issued in Spain for the establishment of a town of four hundred families on the San Antonio River. Years passed, but no settlers came, although the town had been named and a chart had been made showing the location

of the streets and plazas. This town was to be called San Fernando, and it was to be located near the presidio San Antonio de Béxar, not far from the mission San Antonio de Valero.

At last, in April, 1731, the first group of settlers—fifteen families—arrived. They had come from the Canary Islands to Vera Cruz; from Vera Cruz to the City of Mexico; and from that city they had marched northward for seven months! They were footsore and weary,

28

HADEN EDWARDS' PROCLAMATION ORDERED ALL OLD SETTLERS TO PROVE THEIR TITLES TO THEIR LAND OTHERWISE IT WOULD BE SOLD AT AUCTION.

Edward's contract with Mexico specified that he should respect all earlier claims, so he did the honorable thing.

and, we may imagine, none too well pleased with the task that lay before them. They knew nothing about frontier life, but it fell to their lot to become the real pioneers in city building in Texas. Soon they had houses to live in, and had built a church. Before the end of the Spanish period the town was usually referred to as San Antonio, but the town church has retained its original name. On the site of the first little church now stands the San Fernando Cathedral. The presidio, San Antonio de Béxar, which protected the town and the missions, has given its name to the county in which San Antonio is located.

The beginnings of Nacogdoches are quite different from those of San Antonio. In 1763 France gave Louisiana to Spain, and it was therefore no longer necessary for the Spanish to guard East Texas against French attacks. An order was issued in 1773 for the abandonment of the East Texas presidio. At the same

Before his brother received an answer from the Governor, Haden Edwards returned to Nacogdoches, his mission in the United States unsuccessful.

time, all Spanish settlers in that region were ordered to move to San Antonio. There were about five hundred of these settlers who had drifted into the region around present-day East Texas and Western Louisiana, and they were reluctant to leave their homes. As soon as they reached San Antonio, they began begging the governor to allow them to return to their old homes. The governor gave them permission to move as far east as the Trinity River. There the East Texans established a short-lived settlement called Bucareli, in what is now Madison County. But they were never happy there. In 1779, under the leadership of Gil Ybarbo, they abandoned this town and, without permission, moved to the site of the old mission of Guadalupe. Here they established the town of Nacogdoches, and soon built the famous "Old Stone Fort" for their protection. Nacogdoches, which was thus founded only three years after the American Declaration of Independence, soon became an important place. It was the eastern gateway to the province, and a good many of the settlers who came to Texas from the United States after 1820 got their first impressions of their new

Samuel Norris, the alcalde of Nacogdoches, and his followers, the old settlers, went

wild with joy when they heard that Edwards was ordered out of Texas.

homeland at Nacogdoches.

Texas was a Spanish province for a century and a quarter, but not much had been done toward planting European civilization north of the Rio Grande; and even less had been accomplished toward developing the rich natural resources of the country. As late as 1819, a Spanish official reported that Texas was inhabited by "the barbarians and wild beasts," with the exception of the people of San Antonio and La Bahía. The combined population of those towns was not more than 2,500. Nacogdoches, five hundred miles eastward on the frontier, was at that time entirely deserted, although it had once been, and was to be again, a prosperous town.

EARLY INROADS OF ANGLO-AMERICANS

The weakness of Spain's hold on Texas served as a constant invitation for adventurers to push into the country, especially from Louisiana. Philip Nolan was one of the romantic figures who appeared on the Texan scene. For several years he wandered between San Antonio and Natchez, Mississippi, trading with

Bowie was six feet tall, with fierce blue eyes and war-like expression.

the Indians and observing the condition of the country. What his purposes were we cannot be sure, but the Spaniards thought he was a spy of the Americans. His last expedition left Natchez late in 1800. A small Spanish force tried to stop Nolan and his followers at the Washita River in Louisiana, but failed. On they came to the Brazos River, capturing wild horses as they came. They were attacked at their camp, not far from Waco, on March 21, 1801, by a hundred Spanish soldiers from Nacogdoches. There were fourteen fighting men with Nolan, but the battle lasted three hours. Nolan himself was killed, and the others were taken prisoners. Long delay followed the arrest of these men before the Spanish government decided what it should do with them. In 1807 came an order that one out of every five should be hanged. Since there were only nine of them left, it was decided that only one should die. The prisoners threw dice on a drumhead, and Ephriam Blackburn, a Quaker, proved to be the unlucky man. He was

General Barrados with 4,000 men crossed the Atlantic and seized Tampico.

Santa Anna mobilized an army and navy at Vera Cruz and started to dislodge the Spaniards at Tampico.

Santa Anna's fleet blockaded harbor at Tampico and his troops hemmed in the Spaniards.

Without a battle Barrados surrendered to return to Spain with his troops.

In 1829 Anastasio Bustamante usurped the Presidency of Mexico. In the same year Spain made one more effort to recapture her lost provinces.

---

hanged in Chihuahua. One of Nolan's men that lived to play a part in Texas history was Peter Ellis Bean. He remained in Mexico, took part in the revolution against Spain, and in 1825 came back to Texas as a Mexican army officer. He lived at Nacogdoches for many years.

Other expeditions into Texas were made by other adventurers as the years passed. The Gutiérrez-Magee adventure is the most famous, but perhaps the most interesting one was Dr. James Long's expedition. In 1819 this man, who had been an officer in the United States army, placed himself at the head of seventy-five men at Natchez. Three hundred men had joined him before he attacked Nacogdoches, which he captured with ease. Long—"General" Long, as he called himself—declared Texas an independent republic, and official orders and newspapers were published on the printing press that had been brought along. He visited Jean Lafitte, who then was occupying Galveston Island, and offered to make the noted pirate the head of his navy, but Lafitte refused the honor. Then Long pretended

Bradburn, commandant at Anahuac, immediately arrested seventeen colonists.

Bradburn threw the prisoners into a dungeon in the fort. Among them was William B. Travis.

Prisoners demanded to know charges against them.

Prisoners were not released for some time.

A Mexican soldier committed an outrage near Anahuac and the colonists punished him summarily. Bradburn immediately arrested colonists.

---

that he was aiding the Mexicans in their struggle against Spain. On a second expedition, his forces captured La Bahía in October, 1821, but were soon defeated by the Mexican troops. Long was sent a prisoner to Mexico and, after he had been released, was killed by a Mexican soldier.

Long's expedition was interesting, and in a way, important. But its chief contribution to Texas was to bring into this country one of the first, if not the first Anglo-American woman. She was Jane Wilkinson, who had married Dr. Long at Natchez in 1815. After her husband had come into Texas on his expedition, she followed with their children. For two years she remained with him. She held his fort at Bolivar Point during his absence. When the "General" was captured by the Mexicans, Mrs. Long remained in Texas to await his return. Her hardships pass description, but her courage never failed her, even after she learned of her husband's death. She had adopted Texas as her country, and, until she died a very old woman, she was perhaps the most famous of the women of early Texas. The important men

The Texans occupied strategic positions in Anahuac and sent their
leaders to confer with Bradburn on the release of the prisoners.

of Texas visited her home, and she was known affectionately as "the Mother of Texas."

In December, 1820, while General Long was striving to take Texas by force, another American rode a gray horse into San Antonio and dismounted in front of the Governor's palace. He, too, had a scheme to settle Texas. His name was Moses Austin, and he had come to ask permission to settle in Texas three hundred families from the United States. Eventually the permission was given, but Moses Austin had died of pneumonia before he could begin the work. Stephen F. Austin, a young man of twenty-seven, undertook to complete his father's plan to settle Texas by peaceful means. Stephen F. Austin was to become known in history as "the Father of Texas." Jane Long, "the Mother of Texas," whose husband had died attempting to take Texas by force, was to remain in Texas to help the work of the advocate of peace.

Just about the time of the Anahuac affair, politics in Mexico began to
sputter again — we must go back to January 2, 1832.

PRIVATEERS AND PIRATES ON THE TEXAS COAST

During the period of Spain's weakness, and before the settlers from the United States began to arrive, many colorful figures drifted to Texas. Two of these interesting men were Luis Aury and Jean Lafitte. Aury established himself at Galveston Island in 1816, claiming to be a commodore in the service of the group in Mexico which was fighting to overthrow Spanish power. His vessels patrolled the Gulf of Mexico, plundering not only Spanish vessels but any others they could find. An important item in the business of Luis Aury was smuggling Negro slaves into the United States. After he had been on the island for some time, a Spanish adventurer brought two hundred men over to free Mexico from Spanish rule. Aury joined with him, leaving Galveston Island deserted when he sailed away to attack the Mexican coast. The expedition failed, and when Aury's ship came again to Galveston, it was found that another, and greater, pirate had taken possession.

The newcomer was Jean Lafitte, who had already

32

Young Sam Houston worked on the farm and went to school when it was too cold to work.

won a reputation as the most successful pirate along the American coast. He had operated from a base near the mouth of the Mississippi until 1814, when the United States Navy drove him out of business. He and his brother Pierre had once lived in New Orleans, and were known there as blacksmiths. Much of the loot they captured on the Gulf was probably disposed of at their blacksmith shop, which is still pointed out to visitors in New Orleans. The War of 1812 was in progress when the Navy drove Lafitte out of business. The British commander offered Lafitte a high position in the British service if he would turn against the United States. But the pirate, who had his good points, refused. Although charges were pending against him in the courts of New Orleans, he offered his services to General Andrew Jackson, and he and his men helped the United States to win the last battle of the war. The charges against him were never prosecuted, but Lafitte decided to leave the territory of the United States.

In 1817 he had established himself at Aury's old headquarters on Galveston Island, and, like Aury, he professed allegiance to the Republic of Mexico (which did

The Houstons settled in Blount County, Tennessee, eight miles from the Tennessee River.

not exist at the time!). He called his establishment Campeachy, and it was an ideal pirate colony. There was plenty of room for watchtowers, forts, all sorts of buildings, as well as good grazing land for cattle. The bay, with its narrow entrance, behind the island offered safe harbor for the pirates' vessels, and the inlets along the coast afforded convenient hiding places. About a thousand desperate characters joined the settlement, and although Lafitte claimed that he wanted to plunder only Spanish vessels, some of his men began to seize ships flying the United States flag. In 1821 a vessel of the United States Navy called at Galveston Island. Lafitte and his followers loaded their plunder and sailed away.

Not all of the "bad men" of this period lived along the coast. When the United States bought Louisiana in 1803, Spain was too weak to prevent citizens of the United States from crossing over the Sabine River into East Texas. The Sabine was not then, in fact, legally recognized as the boundary line between the United States and Mexico. The United States claimed that the

Before coming to Texas, Sam Houston also served as congressman and governor of Tennessee.

purchase of Louisiana gave her all of the land to the Rio Grande, although she did not attempt to take possession of the territory west of the Sabine. In 1806 after a clash of authority between the generals commanding the United States and Spanish forces along that frontier, an informal agreement was made between them. The territory between the Sabine River and the Arroyo Hondo was declared a neutral ground, over which neither Spain nor the United States should exercise authority. This agreement held until 1819, when the United States gave up her claim to the land west of the Sabine. During these thirteen years all sorts of refugees from justice congregated in this neutral ground, to prey on both American and Spanish settlements.

TEXAS UNDER MEXICO

In 1821 Texas became a part of the new Mexican nation. Texas had served Spain as a buffer province against foreign intrusion. At any time during the last twenty years of her ownership, a strong power could have seized the province.

In December, 1832, Sam Houston crossed the Red River into Texas ostensibly as an adjuster of Indian claims.

Spain did not accomplish as much in Mexico as she might have. Mexico as a whole was rich, and poured the wealth of her mines into the royal treasury. The King of Spain was interested in Mexico principally as a source of revenue, and he did not give much thought to the happiness of the people who lived there. The Viceroy, who ruled the land from Mexico City, was sent over from Spain with full instructions as to what he should do. He was not allowed to form business or social relationships with the people, and he was assisted in governing by other Spaniards. There was little chance for a person born in Mexico, even though of Spanish parents, to become an official. Only one of the sixty-four viceroys, and only one archbishop of Mexico had been born in Mexico. The colonial system was not a good one. It did not satisfy the colonists, and it did not even produce as much revenue for the king as a better one might have produced. But until

In October, 1832, the people of Texas held their first convention. It convened at San Felipe de Austin.

1810 the people appear not to have dreamed of a day when they would be free of Spain.

In 1808, however, Napoleon, who had made himself master of most of Europe, decided to take control of Spain. Loyal Spaniards refused to accept as their king the person Napoleon had set over them. All over Spain they rose up against the French intruder, and in the New World revolutions began.

Miguel Hidalgo, a priest, first raised the standard of revolt in Mexico. On September 16, 1810, he began gathering an army which almost succeeded in capturing Mexico City. September 16 is celebrated as Independence Day in Mexico. Hidalgo was soon captured and executed, and his forces were scattered. Other leaders tried to keep the revolutionary movement alive, but one after another they were captured and executed. The revolt never became really formidable, but there were always enough rebels in the field to make the Spanish authorities uneasy.

Then, in 1820, an unexpected thing occurred. The King of Spain was forced by the army to re-establish a liberal constitution, the provisions of which would

On January 3, 1834, Austin was in Saltillo, Mexico, on his way back to Texas.

apply to the colonies in the New World. This constitution, which had been drawn up in 1812, abolished the special privileges of the army, the church, and the great landholders. When news of this reached Mexico City, the privileged groups determined to separate from Spain rather than submit to this constitution. It was arranged that the Viceroy should appoint Colonel Agustín de Iturbide as commander of a force to exterminate what remained of the rebels. Instead of fighting the rebels, however, Iturbide made an agreement with their leader. The royal army and the rebel forces, this agreement pro-

vided, would fight together for the independence of Mexico! Thus it was that the movement begun by Hidalgo on September 16, 1810, culminated on February 24, 1821, in the so-called Plan of Iguala. The last viceroy from Spain arrived a few months later and was forced to agree to the arrangement.

Although it was expected that some European prince should be made the emperor of independent Mexico, Iturbide managed to get that office for himself. It was perhaps an impossible task that he undertook, that of stabilizing the government of Mexico. He was not a

Lawyers Grayson and Jack, sent by the Colonists to free Stephen F. Austin, set out for Mexico City.

man of great ability, and he failed miserably. Early in 1823 he abdicated. Then confusion in Mexico became even greater. At last a constitutional convention decided that Mexico should be a republic, and in 1824 a constitution similar to that of the United States was adopted. But the Mexicans had had no experience in politics, and this constitution was not well fitted to their needs.

During the administration of the first president of this republic, the vice-president placed himself at the head of a revolution against the president. That set a pattern for the future. Not until long after Texas had ceased to be a part of Mexico did the Mexicans learn the art of governing their country in an orderly manner. Until 1836 governments were changed by military force more often than by elections, and important functions of the government were frequently neglected. The Americans who had settled in Texas were not accustomed to disorder of this sort. Their dissatisfaction with Mexican politics was one of the important reasons for the separation of Texas from the Republic of Mexico.

COLONIZATION ENTERPRISES OF THE AUSTINS

We will understand the story of Texas better if we

In March, 1835, the Legislature of the dual State of Texas and Coahuila met at Monclova.

remember that in 1820, when Moses Austin received permission to settle American families in Texas, Spain still owned Mexico. Before Stephen F. Austin could begin the work, Mexico had become independent under the Plan of Iguala. It was from the government of the Emperor Agustín I (as Iturbide called himself) that permission was obtained to allow the settlers to come in, but before Austin could return to Texas, Agustín I had fallen, and the Republic of Mexico had come into existence.

Once Austin and the other empresarios had got their contracts signed, and had begun to settle Americans in their grants, the people of Texas gave little thought to what was happening in Mexico. The settlers were busy building their homes and clearing the land and planting crops. The means of communication were slow and uncertain, even if the Texans had wanted to keep up with the news from Mexico. The Texans were content to attend to their own business; and the men who followed one another in control of the Mexican government were for many years too much occupied with other matters to give much thought to what was hap-

With the Mexican army of subjugation approaching, the Texans girded themselves for defence.

pending on that northeast frontier of the Republic.

In Texas, during those years, the foundations of an American state were being laid. Moses Austin had asked for permission to bring in three hundred American families, and Stephen F. Austin's first work in Texas was to get them settled on their lands. In 1825 he was given a contract to settle five hundred additional families; in 1827 a hundred more; the next year three hundred more. The news of Austin's work stimulated other men to become empresarios also. Martín de León, a Mexican; Green DeWitt, from Missouri; Haden Edwards; David G. Burnet; Lorenzo de Zavala; Sterling C. Robertson; Ben Milam; McMullen and McGloin, and a host of others sought and received contracts. None of them had the success of Austin. Eighteen colonial contracts were made by the State of Coahuila and Texas between 1825 and 1832. There is scarcely a home in Texas that is not situated upon land that was marked off on the map and assigned to some person who agreed to introduce families into Texas. If all these contracts had been fulfilled, Texas would have had a large population

The strong arm of Santa Anna, self-proclaimed Dictator of Mexico, soon reached to Texas.

before 1836. By modern standards, the population of Texas increased very slowly during the period of American colonization. But if we judge by the population reports for the period before 1820, it grew at an astounding rate. In Austin's colonies alone there were more than 2,000 persons in 1828; 4,248 in 1830; and 5,665 by the middle of the next year. By the end of 1833 Austin had issued land grants to more than a thousand families, and people were still pouring into the colonies.

Who were these people who came into Texas?

Why did they come? And from what parts of the United States did they come? These questions are important but difficult to answer. Many of them were pioneers, who loved the hardships and adventure of the frontier. Others were farmers who had lost everything in the panic of 1819. Then there were professional men — lawyers, physicians, teachers — who for one reason or another came out from the older settlements of the United States. Finally, there were foreigners — French, German, English, Irish — who thought they saw in Texas an opportunity to

After the battle of Concepción, hostilities ceased while the Texans perfected their first state government.

better their condition. They were about the same sort of people that had settled on one frontier after another from the Atlantic to the Pacific.

One of the circumstances that favored the rapid settlement of Texas, and perhaps insured a predominance of steady, trustworthy people, was the Panic of 1819, which followed the War of 1812 in the United States. All over the country people lost everything they owned. Normally those people would have moved to the frontier of the United States "to take up government land. But a new land law in 1820 required cash payment for these lands. That practically closed the public lands of the United States to these home-seekers, just at the time that Texas was being opened to settlement. Thousands of people, then, who ordinarily would have simply moved west in the territory of the United States, pushed across the Sabine and the Red rivers into Mexican territory. No similar enterprise was ever begun at a more auspicious time than the American colonization of Texas. When Stephen F. Austin returned to Natchitoches after his first trip into Texas, he found there nearly three hundred letters of inquiry from Missouri

Between dark and dawn, December 5, 1835, the Texans set out to capture from Mexico the largest city of their commonwealth, San Antonio. Ben Milam was their leader.

and many from Kentucky. "I am convinced that I could take on fifteen hundred families as easily as three hundred if permitted to do so," he wrote.

Practically every state in the Union was represented in the American population of Texas. Louisiana, Alabama, Tennessee, Missouri, and Mississippi contributed the largest numbers; but New York, Kentucky, Ohio, Georgia, Pennsylvania, Virginia, the Carolinas, and even the New England states were also well represented.

A great many of the early settlers of Texas came in response to the advertisements of Stephen F. Austin and other empresarios; but many more came because of the stories of the richness of Texas soil that spread through the United States. One of them—Noah Smithwick—recorded in his reminiscences that he came out to Texas in 1827 because he had heard that the new land was so rich that one could make a living without much effort. It would, he thought, be a lazy man's paradise. Needless to say, he was disappointed in that hope; but he remained to become a useful citizen. Another type may

38

The famous battle of the Alamo is looming as Santa Anna's troops approach San·
Antonio. Before the seige let us look at some of the immortal heroes of that struggle.

---

be represented by Jared E. Groce. He was a Virginian who had operated great plantations in South Carolina, Georgia, and Alabama before he came to Texas in 1822. It is said that he brought a hundred slaves with him from the United States, and that the procession of his slaves, cattle, horses, implements, and household goods looked like a gigantic circus parade. He established himself near Hempstead, and built there a fine home which he called "Bernardo." Men who visited there reported that this establishment was much like the great slave

plantations of the southern portion of the United States.

All sorts of stories used to be told in the United States about the kind of Americans who settled in Texas. It used to be believed that most of them had fled from their old homes to escape punishment for crime, and in some parts of the United States, merchants marked off the unpaid accounts of men who had disappeared suddenly for parts unknown with the letters G. T. T. (Gone to Texas!). A missionary, on her way to Mexico in 1847, wondered what her "parents and friends would

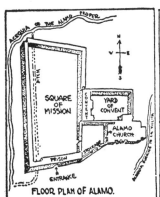

While the Mexican army under Santa Anna was approaching San
Antonio, Colonel Travis took steps to strengthen the Alamo.

---

say if they knew of my mad purpose" to pass through Texas which, she thought was "peopled by outlaws and renegades." There were, of course, undesirable citizens in early Texas. The fact that it was foreign territory made it attractive to people who had fallen afoul of the law in the United States. Most of the settlers, however, were honest, hard-working folk who were anxious to keep bad characters out. At the beginning of the colonization Austin announced:

"No frontiersman who has no occupation than that

of a hunter will be received—no drunkard, nor gambler, nor profane swearer, no idler, nor any man against whom there is even probable grounds of suspicion that he is a bad man . . . Those who are rejected on the grounds of bad character will be immediately ordered out of the country, and . . . should forcible resistance be made by them, the guard will be ordered to fire and kill them."

Travellers almost uniformly reported that the early Texans were hospitable, generous, and honest. "I went

Commandancy of the Alamo.
Bejar, Feby. 24th, 1836—

To the People of Texas & all Americans in the world,

Fellow Citizens & Compatriots—I am besieged, by a thousand or more of the Mexicans under Santa Anna—I have sustained a continued Bombardment & cannonade for 24 hours & have not lost a man—The enemy has demanded a surrender at discretion, otherwise, the garrison are to be put to the sword, if the fort is taken—I have answered the demand with a cannon shot, & our flag still waves proudly from the walls—I shall never surrender or retreat. Then, I call on you in the name of Liberty, of Patriotism, & everything dear to the American character, to come to our aid, with all despatch—The enemy is receiving reinforcements daily & will no doubt increase to three or four thousand in four or five days. If this call is neglected, I am determined to sustain myself as long as possible & die like a soldier who never forgets what is due to his own honor & that of his country—Victory or Death.

WILLIAM BARRETT TRAVIS,
Lt. Col. comdt.

P.S. The Lord is on our side—When the enemy appeared in sight we had not three bushels of corn—We have since found in deserted houses 80 or 90 bushels & got into the walls 20 or 30 head of Beeves—

TRAVIS.

TRAVIS' FAMOUS LETTER TO THE WORLD.

On February 23, Santa Anna, leading the main division of the Texas army, arrived near San Antonio.

all through the country, unarmed and unharmed," wrote one. Another said: "Even men who have been expatriated for fear of justice are here among the last who would be disposed to shield a culprit guilty of a crime against life or property. I can say more: . . . money would be as safe without lock and key as in our own country." He added that stores in Texas were seldom locked, but nobody thought of robbing them.

Thomas J. Pilgrim, the pioneer Texas teacher, said: "That there were some rude and illiterate people among them is no more than may be said of almost any society, and that some were vicious and depraved is equally true, but what there was of evil you saw on the surface, for there was no effort at concealment." That probably is a correct analysis of the case.

BEGINNING OF MEXICAN DISTRUST

For several years after the colonization began, the relations between the American settlers and the Mexican government were happy. Liberal grants of land were given to all who could prove that they had good character and were willing to become Mexican citizens and

On March 3, Colonel Travis made a remarkable speech to his command in the Alamo,
offering his men a chance to escape or certain death.

members of the Catholic Church. At the Mexican capital, as we have seen, the government was in great disorder during this period; but Mexico City was far away, and within Texas the Americans handled their local political affairs about as they pleased. Only when Mexico began to fear that these settlers might some day try to take Texas away from her, did relations become strained.

The first occurrence which made the Mexican government wonder if she had acted wisely in allowing the Americans to settle was the Fredonian

Rebellion in 1826. Haden Edwards had been given a contract to settle eight hundred families around Nacogdoches. There were already a good many Spanish-speaking people in that neighborhood who had lived on the lands for many years, but who had no legal title to their farms. Some Americans had settled there, too, before Edwards received his contract. Nearby were the Cherokee Indians, occupying lands within Edwards' grant. In such a situation, trouble was bound to develop. After some bickering, Edwards unwisely made an alliance with the Chero-

March 4, 1836. Santa Anna's army was now withdrawn some distance from the Alamo.

---

kee Indians, and declared Texas independent under the name of "Fredonia." He said that he proposed to divide the land between his followers and the Cherokees. None of the Americans who were building their homes in the other colonies wanted at that time to go to war with Mexico, and men of Austin's colony aided the Mexican authorities in putting down the rebellion.

It was a small affair, but it made the Mexican government suspicious of the loyalty of the Americans in Texas. From that time on, in spite of the willingness of most of the settlers to live peaceably under Mexican rule, troubles multiplied.

Three years later, President Guerrero declared slavery abolished in the Republic of Mexico. The settlers saw in this decree a deliberate attempt to check immigration from the United States, as well as to embarrass Texas by freeing the thousand or more slaves already there. Austin was able to have the decree set aside; but the next year the Mexican Congress passed the famous Law of April 6, 1830, which once more threw Texas into commotion.

At daybreak, March 6, 1836, Santa Anna ordered the assault on the Alamo.

General Mier y Terán, after a thorough inspection of Texas, had reported to the Mexican government that "the ratio of Mexicans to foreigners is one to ten . . . Texas could throw the whole nation into revolution." Congress took steps to change this situation by passing an act which forbade settlement in Texas of people from adjoining countries and required that visitors should have Mexican passports in order to enter Texas. Empresario contracts were suspended, and it was provided that Mexico might colonize her criminals in Texas.

It was now the colonists' turn to be suspicious of Mex-

ico. They were peaceable people, but they were not willing to have Mexican convicts settled among them, nor did they want to be cut off completely from their friends and relatives in the United States. From 1830 on to the revolution of 1836, neither the Mexicans nor the Texans had much confidence in the motives of the other. Separation was only a question of time.

Soon after the passage of the Law of April 6, 1830, detachments of the Mexican army were stationed at a number of posts in Texas, and at the same time customhouses were opened along the coast and the fron-

CROCKETT WAS FOUND DEAD NEAR THE SOUTH WALL.

BOWIE WAS FOUND DEAD IN HIS COT IN THE NORTHWEST WALL OF THE BARRACKS.

THE ALAMO CHAPEL WAS THE LAST EPISODE OF THIS BLOODY DAY.

TRAVIS' FLAG WAS LOWERED AFTER ALMOST EVERY DEFENDER OF THE ALAMO HAD PERISHED.

The Mexicans flooded the Alamo and fighting became a hand-to-hand carnage.

---

tiers to collect taxes on goods brought in from the United States. Until then, taxes had not been collected on goods imported into Texas. It irritated the colonists to commence paying such taxes; and they disliked especially the thought of paying taxes to support the Mexican forces which had been sent into Texas to keep a watchful eye on the colonists.

Perhaps in the hope of making the Texans feel better about the new deal that was thus inaugurated, the Mexican government appointed an American as commander of the troops at Anahuac, on Galveston Bay.

His name was John Davis Bradburn, and he was a native of Kentucky, although he had been a citizen of Mexico many years. It turned out that the Texans did not have much respect for any American who made his living serving in the Mexican army; and Bradburn seems to have devoted most of his time to irritating the Texans. At best, his job was a difficult one, and the most tactful man might have failed. But Bradburn, so even the conservative Stephen F. Austin thought, was "incompetent to such a command and is half crazy part of the time."

SEÑORA DICKINSON YOU ARE AT LIBERTY TO GO
ABOUT FIFTEEN PEOPLE, MOSTLY WOMEN AND CHILDREN, SURVIVED.

SANTA ANNA ORDERED THE BODIES OF TEXANS BURNED.

THE MEXICAN DEAD WERE BURIED IN A CEMETRY.

COL. JUAN N. SEGUIN, ONE OF THE MANY MEXICAN-TEXANS WHO FOUGHT WITH THE ANGLO-TEXANS, CLAIMS TO HAVE COLLECTED REMAINS OF THE ALAMO DEFENDERS IN AN URN AND BURIED THEM IN A CORNER OF SAN FERNANDO CATHEDRAL.

Santa Anna attacked the Alamo with 3,500 men, losing about 500. Travis had 181 fighting men,
all of whom perished.

He quarrelled first with the town government of Liberty; arrested the land commissioner who was attempting to settle land disputes in the neighborhood; and finally, in the spring of 1832, arrested several prominent citizens of Anahuac because they protested against his acts. The angry colonists determined to make him release the prisoners. They sent men to Brazoria to get two cannon, and, while waiting for the guns, they drew up the famous Turtle Bayou Resolutions.

The Rise of a Feeling of Grievance Against Mexico

These men knew that an attack on Mexican troops, such as they were about to make, would only convince the Mexican authorities that the Texans were rebellious people. They also knew that Santa Anna was then in revolt against the government of President Bustamante, and that he probably would succeed in ousting the president. Some wise man suggested that the Texans ought to declare that this struggle at Anahuac was in favor of

On March 1, 1836, while the siege of the Alamo was in progress, delegates from Texas met in convention at Washington-on-the-Brazos. Of the fifty-nine signers of the Texas Declaration of Independence, only two — Francisco Ruiz and José Antonio Navarro — were born in Texas.

Santa Anna and against Bustamante. Accordingly the men announced to the world that the actions of Bradburn were a sample of the bad government of Bustamante, and that the Texans would give their lives and fortunes in support of "the patriot, Santa Anna"! About a month later, Colonel Mexía, with four hundred men, arrived at the mouth of the Brazos River. Mexía was a supporter of Santa Anna. He had just captured Matamoros, and had come to Texas to put down the rebellion at Anahuac. When he read the Turtle Bayou

Resolutions, and another declaration of loyalty adopted by the citizens of San Felipe, he sailed back to Mexico, convinced that the Texans were true friends of Santa Anna. Bradburn was removed, and most of the Mexican soldiers left Texas.

Now it occurred to the Texans that if the State of Coahuila and Texas could be divided into two states, most of their troubles would end. They were willing for Texas to remain one of the members of the Republic of Mexico, provided the Americans in Texas were given

Sam Houston, commander-in-chief of the armies of the new republic, took charge of his forces at Gonzales.

the right to run the government of the state. When Coahuila and Texas were joined to make a single state, it had been promised that as soon as Texas had sufficient population, she might become a separate state. On October 1, 1832, the Texans sent delegates to a Convention at San Felipe. Fifty-six men sat in this Convention, and they petitioned the Mexican government to grant them separate statehood, as well as to grant a number of other reforms.

Popular conventions, like this one at San Felipe, were

the ordinary American method of presenting complaints to their government, but the Mexicans knew nothing of such procedure. To the Mexicans, any political meeting unauthorized by the government looked very much like treason, and this Texas Convention made them even more suspicious of the designs of the colonists. No additional troops were sent into Texas immediately, however, and the Texans began to think that the election of Santa Anna to the presidency might mean that their requests would be granted. Santa Anna posed as a great

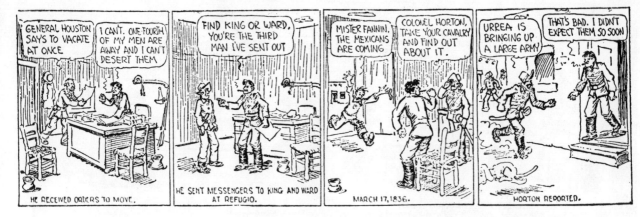

March 14, 1836, Fannin was left in Goliad with about 450 men.

friend of democracy, and he was to take office as president of Mexico on April 1, 1833.

The Texans called another convention to meet at San Felipe on Santa Anna's inauguration day. Most of the delegates were "new men," who had not served in the previous Convention. Among them was Sam Houston, who represented Nacogdoches. A number of petitions, similar in nature to those of 1832, were adopted, and, to hasten the achievement of separate statehood, a constitution for the proposed Mexican state of Texas was adopted. Stephen F. Austin was appointed to pre-

sent the proposed constitution and the petitions to President Santa Anna. Austin had not been in favor of all of the petitions, and had opposed the adoption of the constitution by the convention, but he was unquestionably the best man that could have been sent on this mission. He understood how to deal with the Mexicans, and the Mexican officials had confidence in him.

For six months Austin labored in Mexico City to convince the Mexican government that the requests of the Texans were reasonable and should be granted. He was able to get some of the provisions of the Law of April

After terrible fighting the Mexicans withdrew at nightfall.

6, 1830, changed, but that was all. In despair he wrote to the town council of San Antonio suggesting that the Texans proceed with the establishment of a separate state government. When Mexican officials at San Antonio saw this letter, they informed the officials at Mexico City. At Saltillo, capital of Coahuila-Texas, he was arrested for treason and returned to Mexico City. Not until the summer of 1835 was he released and allowed to return to Texas.

Meantime, more and more of the Texans were becoming convinced that Texas would never prosper as long

as it remained a part of Mexico. A "War Party" was formed, composed of some of the most important men of Texas. This group was small at first but very active. The separation of Texas from Mexico was inevitable, these leaders thought, and the sooner it took place the better. The "Peace Party," on the other hand, continued to hope that some way would be found for Texas to get along with Mexico. Austin had been associated with the "Peace Party" and most of the men of property belonged to it.

Another clash between the Texans and Mexican

Fannin and his men, hopelessly outnumbered on the field of the Coleto, decided to surrender.

---

troops at Anahuac occurred just before Austin reached Texas after his long imprisonment. The night after his arrival at Velasco Austin "walked the beach, his mind oppressed with the gravity of the situation, forecasting the troubles ahead of Texas." The people of Brazoria honored him with a great banquet on September 8, 1835. Austin held the future of Texas in the hollow of his hand that night. All Texas was waiting to hear what he, the former leader of the "Peace Party" would say. Texas would go as Austin went. In plain language he declared against Santa Anna and asked the people to select delegates to a General Consultation. The die was cast! Even the cautious Austin was for action! Soon Austin was writing to a friend: "*I hope to see Texas forever free from Mexican domination of any kind. . . . That is the point we shall end at.*"

Santa Anna, whom the Texans had once thought might aid them in their effort to establish a democratic government, proved a traitor to the liberal cause. Before he had been in the president's office a year, he was making plans to overthrow the Mexican Constitution of

On Palm Sunday, March 27, 1836, the able-bodied men of Fannin's command were marched one-half mile from Goliad.

1824 and make himself dictator of the country. He abolished the state governments, and forced out of office all men who did not promise to aid him in his dictatorship. One after another the states of Mexico fell under his control, until only Zacatecas and Coahuila and Texas offered resistance. Determined to crush those who disputed his authority, the dictator sent armies to crush Zacatecas and Coahuila. In Texas the garrison at San Antonio had been strengthened, and General Cós was instructed first to crush the rebellion in Coahuila, then establish himself at San Antonio de Béxar and attend to the Texans.

THE OPENING OF THE REVOLUTION, 1835

The settlers at Gonzales had a cannon, which had been placed there years before to protect the town against Indians. The commandant at San Antonio demanded the surrender of the cannon, and the men of Gonzales refused to give it up. A company of Mexican soldiers was then sent to get the cannon. On the morning of

*Many sections of the United States were interested in the Texans'
struggle, especially the City of Cincinnati.*

October 2, 1835, a hundred and sixty Texans, armed with their rifles, marched against the Mexican camp. They had the little cannon with them, and across it was draped a sign which read, "Come and Take It!" A Mexican was killed, a Texan was wounded—and the cannon remained at Gonzales.

Sixty years before this, a skirmish had taken place at Lexington between American settlers and British soldiers. That battle marked the beginning of the American revolution. This skirmish at Gonzales is frequently referred to as the *"Lexington of Texas."* By defying the orders of the highest Mexican official in Texas, the colonists were challenging the Mexican nation. The war had begun.

A week later, General Cós, after crushing resistance to Santa Anna south of the Rio Grande, marched his well equipped troops into San Antonio. Fortunately for the Texans, he had left at Goliad, thousands of dollars worth of Mexican military supplies and munitions. These the Texans promptly seized for use against the

President Burnet left his family at New Washington and rode back toward Harrisburg.

Mexicans. The taking of Goliad by the Texans was an important event.

All through the settlements spread the news that Cós and his soldiers had arrived, and that only the prompt organization of an army could save the Texans from the fate of their fellow liberals in Zacatecas and Coahuila. Able-bodied Texans, armed with whatever guns they owned, poured into Gonzales. They constituted the Texan army. Men without uniforms, not formally enlisted, and most of them without actual military experience—although they "could shoot straight and keep their powder dry"— proposed to defeat the best equipped and largest military force that had ever visited Texas. Strangely enough, they succeeded. Under the leadership of Stephen F. Austin, whom they elected general, they marched toward San Antonio and on October 28 won their first victory at Concepción mission. Then they pitched camp about a mile north of the main plaza of San Antonio to await a favorable moment to attack.

Austin was succeeded in command by Edward Burleson, and, as winter came on, it was decided by the offi-

On April 14, Houston was at Donoho's, just across the Brazos, when
he heard that Santa Anna had taken Harrisburg and New Washington.

cers to withdraw to Goliad or Gonzales and wait for better weather before attacking the Mexican stronghold. But on December 4, one of the Texans shouted to the men in front of the headquarters: "Who will go with Old Ben Milam into San Antonio?" Three hundred men volunteered at once, and by dawn the next day the strange battle of San Antonio had begun. With battering rams the Texans broke through the walls of the adobe houses, and slowly dug their way into the heart of the city. On the night of the 8th they reached the

military plaza, and the next morning General Cós moved his forces into the walls of the Alamo and asked for terms. He surrendered, and marched 1,100 of his men back into Mexico, after they had agreed not to resist the re-establishment of the Federal Constitution of 1824. Two hundred of the Mexican soldiers chose to remain with the Texans. When Cós's army crossed the Rio Grande on Christmas day, not a Mexican soldier remained on the soil of Texas.

Texas had not yet declared her independence. The

The Texans wanted to fight. Colonel Sidney Sherman asked
permission to take out a troop of cavalry.

Consultation, which met at San Felipe on November 3 —while the Texan army was in camp near San Antonio —declared that the Texans were fighting for the principles of the Mexican Constitution of 1824, which Santa Anna had destroyed. The vote was thirty-three in favor of this declaration, and fifteen in favor of independence. That probably represents the division of opinion among the people of Texas at that time. This Consultation also set up a g   ernment for the proposed Mexican state of Texas. Henry Smith was elected provisional governor;

James W. Robinson, provisional lieutenant governor; Sam Houston, major general of the army; and Stephen F. Austin, W. H. Wharton, and Branch T. Archer were appointed commissioners to the United States.

This provisional government did not work well. The governor quarreled with his council, and the army would not recognize General Houston as their commander. By January, 1836, Texas had no government. The governor suspended the council, and the council impeached the governor, and the people of Texas ceased

At 3:00 P.M., April 21, 1836, Houston gave the command to attack.

to obey orders of either of them. This, and other developments, indicated to thoughtful Texans that another Convention would have to meet, to decide the future of the region. Half way measures had failed. Mexico would certainly attempt to punish Texas for the humiliation of Cós's army. Santa Anna had been victorious in every other part of Mexico. He would come personally to Texas at the head of a great army to force the colonists either to submit to his dictatorship or to flee beyond the Sabine River. The Texans must submit or fight for their rights.

The Convention met at Washington-on-the-Brazos, which a visitor thought was "a rare place to hold a national convention in. It is laid out in the woods," he continued, "about a dozen wretched cabins and shanties constitute the city; not one decent house in it." The delegates met in an unfinished carpenter shop, without doors or windows, and many of them slept on the ground under the trees. A norther swept down as the meeting opened. On the second day of the session, March 2, 1836, the Declaration of Independence was adopted by a unanimous vote. Having declared themselves free

While Houston was advancing, Santa Anna's army was enjoying siesta.

of Mexico, these Texans wrote the Constitution for the Republic of Texas, took measures to insure the winning of the war, and elected officers to serve until an election could be held.

David G. Burnet, a native of New Jersey who had been in Texas many years, was elected president ad interim; Lorenzo de Zavala, a distinguished Mexican who had fled to Texas to escape Santa Anna's wrath, was made vice-president; and Sam Houston was made commander-in-chief of all of the military forces of the Republic.

Now Texas had a government that its people could

support, and one that could deal with other nations. It came not a minute too soon. Santa Anna, at the head of more than six thousand troops, had already marched into Texas. Late in February the vanguard of his army reached San Antonio. William B. Travis, James Bowie, David Crockett, and a small band of other patriots were determined to hold the Alamo even if it cost them their lives. "We consider death preferable to disgrace, which would be the result of giving up a post so dearly won, and thus opening a door for the invaders to enter the sacred territory of the colonies," they declared.

With a ferocity rarely equalled in military annals the Texans completely routed the Mexicans.

THE WINNING OF INDEPENDENCE

On February 24, as the Mexican forces began to surround the old mission, Travis sent out his heroic appeal: "To the People of Texas and all Americans in the World." Soon the siege began. Santa Anna himself arrived and took charge of operations on March 2, the very day that the Texans at Washington-on-the-Brazos were adopting the Declaration of Independence. At dawn on March 6 the battle of the Alamo was over. Only one man of the Texas force is known to have survived to tell the story, but there may have been one or two others, in addition to several women and children.

News of this disaster spread panic through the settlements. The Convention at Washington finished its business as soon as possible and the members hurried off to protect their families. Settlers gathered their families together and rushed toward the Sabine River, hoping to reach the territory of the United States before Santa Anna's forces overtook them. This was called the Runaway Scrape.

One division of the Mexican army, under General Urrea, had marched up from Matamoros through the San Patricio region, annihilating detachments of the Texan army as it came. Urrea captured Refugio, then

The captured Santa Anna was taken before Houston and Secretary Rusk beneath Houston's outdoor headquarters, the Live Oak tree.

surrounded Colonel Fannin's command near Goliad. After a desperate fight against overwhelming odds, the Texans surrendered on March 20 and returned to Goliad as prisoners of the Mexicans. There, at daybreak on March 27, they were marched out in squads and shot down by order of Santa Anna. This came three weeks after the fall of the Alamo. Nothing more was needed to arouse the Texans. "Remember the Alamo! Remember Goliad!" was to be the battle cry at San Jacinto.

Houston had assumed command of the army at Gon-

zales on March 11. Less than four hundred men, poorly armed and ignorant of military training, constituted the force with which he was expected to defeat Santa Anna's well-equipped soldiers. It appeared to be a hopeless undertaking. News of the fall of the Alamo came soon after Houston reached Gonzales. Houston decided to move eastward rather than meet the enemy on that frontier. Men joined, and left, the army as the retreat to the east continued. There were six hundred men with him when he reached the Colorado River; a little later

On April 28th, President Burnet and his cabinet arrived at San Jacinto
Field from Galveston, where they had taken refuge.

there were about 1,400. When he came to the Brazos River, his force had dwindled to half that number. During the two weeks that the army camped near Hempstead, recruits brought the Texan strength to about 1,300. Everybody in Texas began to wonder what Houston was planning.

There was a rumor that he intended to retreat across the border into the United States. Even the president and the secretary of war were worried. "I consulted none— held no councils of war. If I err, the blame is mine." That

was the only information they could get from General Houston. Santa Anna thought that the Alamo and Goliad massacres had broken the resistance of the Texans. He scattered his forces widely for the purpose of sweeping leisurely through the country to exterminate the Texan troops that remained. On April 20, the troops under Santa Anna's personal command found themselves face to face with the Texans under Houston on Buffalo Bayou. The remainder of the Mexican army was scattered about and many miles away. Some shots

On June 1st Santa Anna was placed on board the ship "Invincible," which was to sail to Vera Cruz.

were exchanged between the opposing forces on the 20th of April, but no battle took place.

On April 21, 1836, at San Jacinto, one of the most decisive and at the same time one of the strangest battles in history was fought. The officers of the Texan army decided to delay attacking the Mexicans, and a council of Mexican officers had decided not to attack the Texans until the next day. Santa Anna, who now had more than 1,150 men in his camp, lay down under the trees for a *siesta*. The Texan soldiers, who had not yet learned much about military discipline, voted to set aside the

decision of their officers and to attack the Mexicans that afternoon. The Mexicans were taken completely by surprise. Santa Anna wrote afterwards: "I was sleeping deeply when the din and fire of battle awoke me. I immediately became aware that we were being attacked and that great disorder prevailed." The Texans were charging through his camp like mad men, shouting "Remember the Alamo! Remember Goliad!" and soon Antonio López de Santa Anna, dictator of Mexico and commander-in-chief of all her armies, was plunging through the tall grass in an effort to save his life. The

One of the first acts of President Houston was to visit Santa Anna,
imprisoned on a ranch at Orozimbo.

---

battle was over in twenty minutes or less; what followed was in remembrance of the Alamo. General Houston reported that six hundred and thirty Mexicans were killed, two hundred and eight wounded, and seven hundred and thirty captured. Two of the Texans were killed, and twenty-three of them wounded. The Independence of Texas, declared at Washington on March 2, was won at San Jacinto on April 21.

The Republic of Texas

The Republic of Texas now became a reality. For ten years, from 1836 to 1846 when she became one of the states of the United States, she maintained her independence. Her white population was only about 30,000 when she declared her independence, and hardly more than 100,000 ten years later. Besides David G. Burnet, who was ad interim president, Houston served as president from 1836 to 1838 and from 1841 to 1844. Mirabeau B. Lamar, who came to Texas to be a soldier in the Revolution, was chief executive from 1838 to 1841; and Anson Jones, a physician from New England, who

Houston began his administration with an admirable cabinet and with
great promise of constructive results.

---

had lived in Texas since 1833, was the last president of the Republic. It was Jones, first as secretary of state and then as president, who conducted the difficult negotiations that resulted in annexation.

J. Pinckney Henderson was chosen first governor of the state of Texas, and on a cool February day in 1846 he was inaugurated at Austin. The ceremony took place in front of the rude log house which had been the capitol of the Republic. No scene quite like this is recorded in history. A free and independent republic was voluntarily giving up its sovereignty in order to become a part of another nation. President Jones delivered his last official address to the throng that had gathered to witness the ceremony: "The great measure of annexation, so earnestly desired by the people of Texas, is happily consummated . . . The lone star of Texas, which ten years since arose amid clouds over fields of carnage and obscurely shone for a while, has culminated, and, following an inscrutable destiny, has passed on and become forever fixed in that glorious constellation—the Ameri-

Houston finally resorted to Indian cunning to subdue his mutinous army.

can Union. The final act of this great drama is now performed. The Republic of Texas is no more!"

There were tears in the eyes of many of the weather-beaten listeners as the president reverently lowered the tri-color flag of the Republic of Texas for the last time. But as the flag of the American Union took its place and caught the breeze, shouts resounded as the cannon roared.

TEXAS, THE NEW STATE

Governor Henderson, at the outbreak of the Mexican War, was granted a leave of absence by the legislature to take command of all the Texas troops in the United States army. He had the rank of major general. On his staff were Mirabeau B. Lamar, Edward Burleson, Henry L. Kinney, and Edward Clark. Among the soldiers was a troop of Texas cavalry commanded by Colonel Albert Sidney Johnston, who later became one of the most famous of Confederate officers. There was also a Texas German regiment under the command of August Buchel. Many other noted Texans were officers in the army during the Mexican War. Texas furnished nearly eight thousand men, a greater number in proportion to

President Lamar proposed to extend Texas' boundaries over New Mexico.

its population than any other state in the Union. When the treaty of peace was signed on February 2, 1848, at Guadalupe Hidalgo, approximately sixty-five miles from Mexico City, Texas was directly interested because the Rio Grande was designated as the official boundary between Texas and Mexico.

The frontier was wild and Indian depredations grew in fury. The vast stretches of the new state, combined with the meager means of communication, made it very difficult for civilization to push forward from the towns and cities. The United States government established forts and army posts in all sections. At one of the posts was a very popular young lieutenant. His name was Robert E. Lee. There were many other young officers stationed at the posts, who later fought against each other in the Civil War.

Politics also began to be the intense topic of the times. Public offices had increased, the population grew by leaps and bounds, and famous statesmen held the stage of public interest. George T. Wood followed Hender-

SEÑORES, LAY DOWN YOUR ARMS. YOU ARE PRISONERS OF WAR.

THEY WERE IMMEDIATELY CAPTURED BY GOVERNOR ARMIJO.

THERE'RE 2,000 MILES MORE OF IT, BOYS

OH, MY FALLEN ARCHES!

THE TEXANS WERE WALKED OVERLAND TO MEXICO CITY.

THE TEXANS WERE IMPRISONED AND SUFFERED GREATLY.

THIS LIGHT BLINDS ME

AT MUCH EXPENSE AND TROUBLE THE SURVIVORS WERE RELEASED.

The Sante Fe expedition reached San Miguel, N.M., in August, 1841.

son as Governor in 1847. In 1849, Peter Hansboro Bell, who participated in the Battle of San Jacinto, became governor. He was followed by Elisha M. Pease in 1853. Hardin R. Runnels followed Pease. Then, in 1859, Sam Houston, who had returned to popular favor, became governor of Texas.

Sam Houston and his close friend, Thomas J. Rusk, were chosen by the state legislature to be the first United States senators from Texas. Mirabeau B. Lamar became United States minister to Nicaragua in 1857.

Anson B. Jones, Texas' last president, hoped to be elected to the United States Senate in 1857, but was not chosen by the legislature. In the old Capitol Hotel in Houston on January 7, 1858, Jones remarked to a friend, "Here in this house, twenty years ago, I commenced my political career in Texas as a member of Congress, and here I would like to close it." Within an hour a shot rang out in his room, and when the door was opened Anson Jones was found dying by his own hands.

Sam Houston was not pleased at the methods of the United States authorities in handling the Indian

RUSK, I'VE BEEN IN THIS PLACE BEFORE

SAM HOUSTON AND T.J RUSK WENT TO WASHINGTON AS THE FIRST SENATORS.

WE'LL HAVE TO FIGHT AGAIN, ODIE.

THE MEXICANS CLAIM THE NUECES IS THE BORDER AND WE THINK THE RIO GRANDE IS

HOSTILITIES SEEMED IMMINENT WITH MEXICO.

A SPLENDID PIECE OF MACHINERY

GENERAL ZACHARY TAYLOR USA, WAS STATIONED AT CORPUS CHRISTI.

THE DISPUTED TERRITORY.

On December 29, 1845, Texas was officially annexed to the United States.
J. Pinckney Henderson was elected first governor of the State of Texas.

problem. He once said that for one hundred thousand dollars a year he would guarantee to keep peace along the whole line of Texas and New Mexico, the defense of which was then costing the government six million dollars annually.

The Comanches were the chief troublemakers for the settlers in Texas. Choctaws, Chickasaws, and Kickapoos from the Indian Territory also caused trouble. It was very difficult to pursue them north of Red River and punish them.

Many reservations were set aside for Indians in Texas, but none very effective in curbing their

activities and trouble to the settlers. It was found that the Texas Rangers constituted the best force for the suppression of Indian raids, although they cost the state a great deal of money. The congress of the United States finally voted funds with which to aid Texas in carrying on the work of the Rangers.

THE CIVIL WAR

The Indian troubles were still a hindrance to the settling of the outlying stretches of the state when the rumblings of slavery and secession descended upon the South. Sympathy of the vast majority of Texans was

NEGRO SLAVES WERE PART OF TEXAS HISTORY. MANY FOUGHT VALIANTLY FOR TEXAS INDEPENDENCE. OTHERS WORKED THE FIELDS AND SOME WERE COMPANIONS OF THEIR MASTERS. ONE OF THE MOST FAMOUS WAS "RICHMOND" WHO ACCOMPANIED MOSES AUSTIN WHEN HE MOVED FROM MISSOURI TO TEXAS.

with the people of the Old South. Old Southern customs and life had become a part of the new state and huge plantations had their quota of slaves. The question shook the foundations of the state government. Sam Houston was opposed to secession and refused to call a convention when Lincoln was seen as the next president.

The people, through their representatives, held a convention at Austin on January 28, 1861. Houston had already called the legislature in session. He advised caution in the matter of withdrawing from the union. But the legislature voted to recognize the authority and legality of the convention, and instructed it to submit the question of secession to the people. The convention adopted an ordinance of secession by a vote of 166 to 7. Texas had cast her lot with the Confederacy.

On March 16 the convention declared the office of governor vacant and directed Lieutenant-Governor Edward Clark to assume the executive powers. The Constitution of the Confederacy was ratified on March 23, and three days later the new state officials were functioning.

Within a month Texas had furnished 8,000 men for

THE FIRST BATTLES OF THE WAR WERE ON TEXAS SOIL AT PALO ALTO AND RESACA DE LA PALMA.

ON FEBRUARY 2, 1848, THE UNITED STATES ARMY ENTERED MEXICO CITY AND THE WAR WAS OVER.

GEORGE T. WOOD
TEXAS, NOW SECURE, PROCEEDED TO ELECT ITS SECOND GOVERNOR.

RAILROADS BEGAN TO PIERCE THE INTERIOR OF THIS MIGHTY STATE.

General Taylor crossed the Nueces and marched to the Rio Grande and hostilities commenced.

the Confederate army. Preparations were hastily made to take an active part in the war. The Confederate conscript law brought into active service all men between eighteen and thirty-five who could not get exemptions or hire substitutes.

Because of her location, few major battles were fought in Texas. But one distinction can be handed Texas. Near Brownsville the final battle of the Civil War was fought. At Palmito Ranch on May 13, 1865. Colonel Ford defeated 800 Federals and to his surprise learned that Robert E. Lee had surrendered on April 9, more than a month before! When the Civil War began there were many persons who were Unionists. Most of them supported the Confederacy. Many of the soldiers of Texas opposed secession, but were intensely sympathetic towards the South and her life and tradition.

It is recorded that, save for the drain upon her manpower and material resources, Texas suffered little by the war. She was the only Confederate state that was not overrun by the invaders. Good crops were harvested every year, and business never wavered in its growth. The Federals were never able to stop Texas trade across the Rio Grande. At the end of the war Texas had more money and foodstuffs than all the rest of the South put together.

Texas voted to secede from the Union on February 23, 1861. After fighting with the Confederacy in the Civil War, Texas returned to the Union, and in 1869 adopted a new constitution.

RECONSTRUCTION

The return of thousands of homeless soldiers and the resultant confusion in governmental affairs combined to make conditions trying for a few years. Life had to be re-adjusted and a system of state government worked out to the best interests of the people. The triumphant North, industrialized, did not understand the agrarian South and Southwest. Frontier individualism was the order of the day in Texas. The problems of economic and social standards became acute between the North and the South and their influence found its mark in the readjustment of state governmental affairs. Texas was finally readmitted to the Union on March 30, 1870, and civil authority was transferred to officers elected by the people.

In 1876 Texas adopted a still newer constitution and the foundations were laid for peace and prosperity.